THE LEGEND OF
ODYSSEUS

Peter Connolly

To my son Matthew

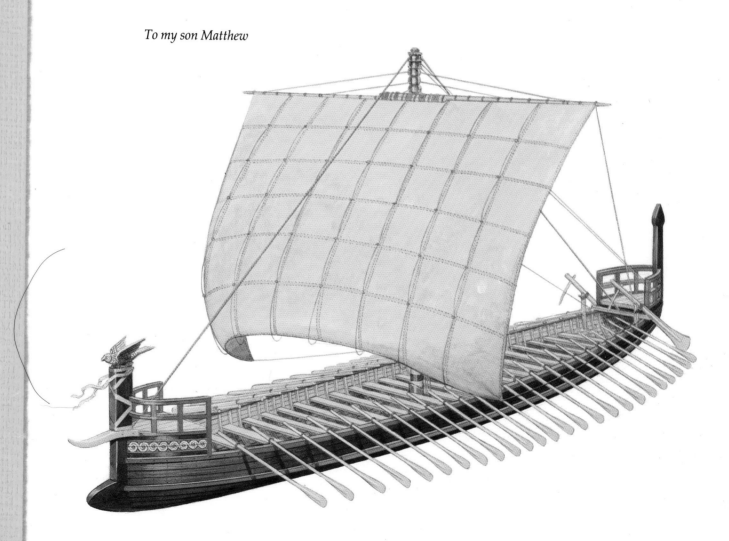

Oxford University Press

Contents

Foreword   3

1 ALL BECAUSE OF A GIRL
The oath   4
The heroes assemble   6
A narrow escape   8
The quarrel   10
Empires in Chaos   12
Agamemnon's Citadel at Mycenae   14
Ships   16

2 DAYS OF DEATH
The duel   18
A battle with the gods   20
Ajax and Hector   22
Zeus intervenes   24
The battle for the ships   26
The Warrior: Helmets   28
The Warrior: Body Armour and Weapons   30
The Warrior: Other Armour, Shields and Chariots   32
Religion and Burial Rites   34

3 DAYS OF SORROW
Patroclus   36
Hector's last fight   38
A double disaster   40
The wooden horse   42
Troy: The Plain   44
Troy: The Excavations   46
Troy: The Siege   48

4 THE GREAT ADVENTURE
The return of the Heroes   50
Penelope   52
A one-eyed giant   54
The valley of death   56
A whirlpool and a monster   58
The Voyages of Odysseus   60
Old Nestor's Palace at Pylos   62

5 THE HOMECOMING
Telemachus returns   64
Impending doom   66
Penelope offers a challenge   68
The final reckoning   70
Men, Women and Costume   72
Dating and Domestic Life   74
Ithaca: The Home of Odysseus   76
The Trojan War: FACT OR FICTION?   78

Index   79

Foreword

'It *must* have looked like this!' Eyes gleaming, Peter Connolly banged the pad on his rucksack for emphasis. Swiftly the pen sketched a city with walls and towers and a columned palace beetling over the plain. My first experience of Peter's enthusiasm — and his remarkable ability to bring the past back to life — could not have been more fitting. We were sitting in a field of cotton below the devastated mound which — so most people think — was once Troy, Hisarlik in north-west Turkey. Back home in England that sketch became a haunting painting of the doomed city (see page 39) which excited and moved everyone who saw it: this, surely, was indeed what it had been like!

Peter Connolly is the most exciting and gifted illustrator now working on the ancient world. Over the last few years he has produced a string of marvellously visualised and detailed reconstructions of ancient life and, especially, of ancient warfare. Now he has turned to the greek legends of Troy, adopting an intriguing approach by attempting to combine the legends — and above all, Homer — with the archaeological evidence for the world to which they dimly hark back, the so called Age of the Heroes, the 13th century BC, when many think the Trojan War took place. Here, at last, you can see Achilles and Hector with the armour and wargear they would have worn had they existed. But *did* they exist?

Increasingly, modern scholars are prepared to believe that something like the Trojan War really took place — perhaps in c1275–60 BC — one of a number of forays by mainland Greeks against the shores of Anatolia. But as yet we do not know whether any of the heroes Peter has so vividly brought to life — Achilles, Hector, Ajax, Paris — were real people. A sensational new discovery may cast fresh light on the old tales. In 1984, on the coast west of Troy, German archaeologists began to excavate a huge Bronze Age tumulus, Besiktepe, apparently the mound identified by the ancients as the tomb of Achilles. Here, by mid 1985, 56 burials and cremations had been discovered with Greek pottery and grave goods from the traditional period of the Trojan War. Could it be that the burial place of the heroes has, after all, been found? Now read on!

MICHAEL WOOD

1

ALL BECAUSE OF A GIRL

The oath

The oath had been sworn and would have to be kept. There seemed to be no way out of it. Much had changed since Odysseus had made that promise. He was now king of Ithaca and married, with a baby son.

The rocky island of Ithaca lay off the west coast of Greece. Its densely wooded hills were alive with deer and other game which Odysseus loved to hunt. At that very time he was training a new dog which he had called Argus after the mythical hero with a hundred eyes who saw all and missed nothing. Argus was hardly more than a puppy but he had the makings of a great hunting dog.

Odysseus' passion for hunting once almost cost him his life. Some years earlier he had been savagely gored by a wild boar, and the wound had left a ragged scar above his knee. But this had not put him off. He was a superb marksman and would sometimes display his skill by shooting an arrow through a line of twelve axes without hitting one of them.

He was also a great story teller. He loved to hold an audience spellbound. Some might call him a liar but his friends knew him better than that. He just liked to improve a story, and if sometimes the truth became a little lost – well, that was just unfortunate.

Odysseus was a thick-set man, about thirty years old. His wife, Penelope, was hardly more than half his age. Before Odysseus brought her back to Ithaca he built a bedroom for them both around the trunk of an old olive tree which he had trimmed and smoothed down. The trunk formed the head of a richly decorated bed which he had made with his own hands. This room was their secret place which no-one else was allowed to enter.

When only a youngster, Odysseus had been savagely gored by a wild boar in a hunting accident. This had left a jagged scar above his knee.

To return to that oath – that stupid promise made so long ago; it had all happened because of a girl – Helen, the most beautiful girl in Greece. Every young man had dreamed of marrying Helen. Odysseus had been no exception. He had gone to Sparta to declare his love but he was not surprised when Helen's father chose Menelaus, the king of Sparta, to be Helen's husband. After all, Menelaus' brother, Agamemnon, was king of Mycenae, and the most powerful ruler in Greece.

But the real cause of all the trouble to come was Hera, the queen of the gods, and two other goddesses, Athena and Aphrodite. They were very vain and had a furious quarrel over which of them was the most beautiful. Finally they decided to let a man settle their argument. Their judge was to be Paris, son of the King of Troy.

Now Paris hoped that if he chose Aphrodite, the goddess of love, she would make Helen fall in love with him. And this is what happened. Helen eloped with Paris and took a lot of her husband's treasure with her. By the time Menelaus discovered the loss, the two lovers had disappeared.

At the time of Helen's betrothal many of the suitors had protested that their love was greater than that of Menelaus. To avoid any trouble, Helen's father had insisted that they all swear an oath that if any one took Helen away from Menelaus, the others would unite to get her back. But the trouble was, nobody knew where she had gone.

Years passed. Then a few months before our story begins, Paris returned to Troy, bringing the beautiful Helen with him. This was the news that was now worrying Odysseus. The oath had been sworn and now he and all the other disappointed suitors were being called upon to honour it.

The heroes assemble

The kingdom of Ithaca was right on the edge of the Greek lands. Because it was so isolated Odysseus hoped he would be able to avoid the king of Sparta's summons. But Menelaus and his brother Agamemnon were already touring Greece demanding that all the kings and princes honour their vow without delay.

Odysseus tried every way he could to avoid going. He even pretended to be mad, but they saw through his act. Honour prevented him making an outright refusal and finally he agreed to go. He gathered 600 men and with twelve warships sailed right round the southern tip of Greece. He passed the treacherous and stormy Cape of Malea, and turned north to Aulis. Here all the great warriors of Greece had gathered.

Aulis lies in the long channel behind the island of Euboea. The narrow strait forms a natural haven against the northerly winds that lash the coast of Greece. As Odysseus sailed up the channel he saw the hundreds of black hulled ships dragged up the beaches well clear of the water. He spotted those belonging to Agamemnon and Menelaus, but there were many others that he did not recognise.

Odysseus beached his ships and made his way to the headquarters. Agamemnon, being both Menelaus' brother and the most powerful Greek king, had naturally taken command of the expedition. The two brothers were well pleased with the muster. The great Diomedes, king of Argos, was there, and also the mighty Ajax, prince of Salamis. Ajax was famed for his size and enormous strength. He and Diomedes were the greatest warriors of southern Greece. Both were already famous, and the bards sang of their exploits.

There was another great hero – in fact the greatest of all, the golden haired Achilles. He came from the north where Greek and barbarian mingled. He was a fearless warrior and the greatest runner of his time. No more than a boy, already his skill was becoming legendary throughout Greece. But Achilles was more than human; although his father was a man his mother was a goddess, the sea nymph Thetis. Achilles was far too young to have courted Helen but he loved war and would not have missed this expedition for anything.

In Agamemnon's tent Odysseus also met the famous king of Pylos, old Nestor. Thirty years earlier the old king would have played a leading role in such an expedition but age had robbed him of his strength. Now he could act only as an adviser. As such he was honoured, although he often bored the other heroes with endless accounts of the battles of his youth.

Ajax

Old Nestor

The Trojans had had warning that the invasion was coming, and were making their own preparations; repairing the walls of the city and stocking up with food. They were massively outnumbered by the Greeks but they too had heroes. Paris, the cause of the war, could not be counted amongst these. He was terrified of hand-to-hand combat and liked to stay in the background, using a bow to snipe at his enemies. His brother Hector, and Aeneas were the real heroes of Troy, and worthy opponents of the Greeks. Hector was the very backbone of the Trojan forces – always in the front line urging his men on. Only Achilles was a match to him. The other hero, Aeneas, like Achilles was a half god, his mother being none other than the goddess of love, Aphrodite.

When all the Greek forces had assembled, sacrifices were offered to avoid upsetting the gods and every man swore solemnly that he would not return until Helen had been recovered. The ships were then dragged down to the water and the great armada set out.

Diomedes

Menelaus

Aeneas

Achilles

Odysseus

Agamemnon

Hector

The heroes of the Trojan War. Homer tells us that Achilles had golden hair, Menelaus red and Odysseus auburn hair. He tells us little else about the appearance of his heroes except for the huge size of Ajax. But he gives a detailed description of Agamemnon's highly decorated armour.

A narrow escape

The Trojans saw the fleet approaching and attacked the Greeks as they tried to land. Hector, who was in command, fought with great courage but they were outnumbered ten to one. As more and more Greeks crowded ashore the Trojans were gradually forced back from the water's edge.

Achilles had beached his ships further up the coast but when he saw the fighting he dashed along the shore and threw himself into the thick of the battle. The Trojans, terrified by the very sight of him, soon fled for the safety of the city.

The Greeks did not pursue. They collected their dead and established a camp on the shore. Agamemnon called the council together and it was agreed that the two sides should try to settle matters peacefully before there was too much bloodshed. Odysseus was already renowned for his silver tongue. When he was asked if he could go up to the city with Menelaus he accepted willingly. If anyone could

persuade the Trojans to hand over Helen and her treasure it was Odysseus.

The two men were filled with a mixture of apprehension and excitement as they set out across the plain. The north wind, heavy with dust, howled around them blowing their long hair in their faces. Ahead of them they could see the city perched at the end of a long spur, its massive limestone walls and towers sparkling in the morning sun, and crowned by the palace rising high above everything.

As they approached they were met by Antenor, a member of the Trojan council. He took them through the Scaean Gate with its huge flanking tower and they made their way up the steep paved street towards the palace. Odysseus noted all he saw: the terraces rising like giant steps, the large houses of the rich built on the terraces and the crude hovels of the poor crowded up against the inside of the walls.

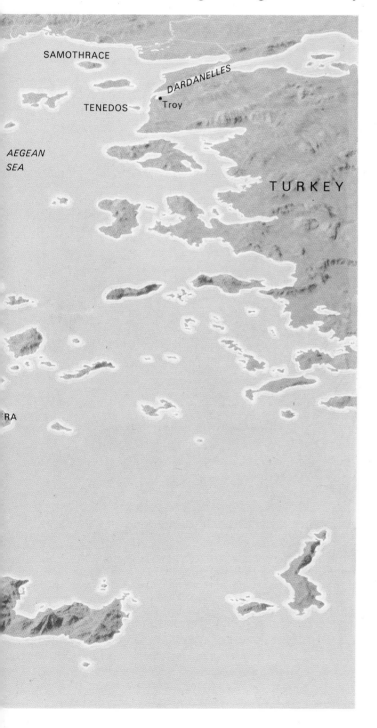

Antenor escorted them to the council chamber where Menelaus, tall and imposing, was invited to put his case. He spoke clearly and simply while the council listened politely but offered no comment. Then Odysseus rose to his feet. He was much shorter than Menelaus and looked far less impressive. He stood, his head bowed in thought, with his ambassador's staff held stiffly in front of him. Some of the council began to snigger but when he glanced up from under his shaggy brows and his rich voice filled the council chamber they felt compelled to listen. Odysseus argued the case brilliantly but for all his eloquence he was unable to persuade them.

Tempers were running high. On the beach, many Trojans had been killed, and their families were thirsting for revenge.

'Why didn't you send an embassy before you declared war?' one of the councillors demanded. 'Yesterday's bloodshed could have been avoided. No, we know you Greeks of old. You are spoiling for a fight.'

Paris' supporters were quick to exploit the worsening situation and angry voices began to shout for blood. Soon the two Greeks were in danger of being torn to pieces. Odysseus looked around him for a way of escape. At that moment all eyes were focussed on those who were shouting for blood. It could only be a matter of moments before attention turned to Menelaus and himself.

Suddenly someone grabbed Odysseus by the arm. He swung round with fist raised to see Antenor, the councillor who had escorted them to the meeting. The Trojan hurried them towards a small side exit which brought them down into a yard behind the council chamber. He guided them along the back streets and out of the gates where their horses were waiting for them. It had been a narrow escape.

The Greeks, furious at the treatment of their ambassadors, decided to launch an all-out attack on the city. But the massive walls were too much for them. They were driven back with heavy casualties and Agamemnon had to call off the assault.

Hopes of an easy victory began to fade. The Greeks realized that they would never take the city by storm, and the Trojans made it quite clear that they were not prepared to fight in the open. So the Greeks decided to destroy the crops and burn the surrounding villages, believing that the Trojans would have to come out and defend their neighbours. They were wrong. They only succeeded in driving the country people into the city and increasing the numbers of its defenders.

The quarrel

Months dragged on into years and still Troy stood. The Greeks still hoped that they could force the Trojans to come out and fight. They widened the area of the war, launching far ranging raids up and down the coast which left a trail of destruction wherever they went. As the raids ranged farther and farther afield so more and more people flocked to join the Trojan side. Raiding continued year after year until it almost became a way of life and the purpose of the war seemed all but forgotten.

Amongst a batch of female captives brought back from one of the raids was the daughter of a priest of Apollo. She had been captured by Achilles.

Agamemnon, as commander-in-chief, had first choice of the spoils of war, and he wanted the priest's daughter. When the priest himself came to the Greek camp offering a large ransom for his daughter Agamemnon was unmoved. The king turned down the offer and drove the old man out of the camp. But Apollo was quick to avenge his priest by sending a plague to scourge the army. The animals began to die almost at once and then the soldiers fell sick too.

The plague raged for nine days. Everywhere smoke rose from the funeral pyres as the soldiers burned their dead comrades. Achilles called an emergency assembly and accused Agamemnon of causing the disaster. And the army insisted that the priest's daughter be sent back. Agamemnon turned on Achilles in fury. 'If I must give up the girl,' he shouted 'you must replace her with another just as beautiful. How about Briseis, the girl you chose? Yes, I'll have her.'

Achilles was livid. He reached for his sword and would have killed Agamemnon on the spot if the goddess Athena had not grabbed him by the hair and held him back. Achilles swung round angrily. He was the only one who could see the goddess. She spoke gently but firmly. 'Put away your sword, Achilles. Cut him with words. Your day of revenge will come.'

Achilles turned on Agamemnon again shouting abuse at him. 'You miserable scoundrel. Take the girl if you must but I warn you, this is the last order I shall ever take from you. One day you will need me desperately but you will have to fight without me and without my men. This I swear. When Hector stands victorious, surrounded by Greek dead, you will regret this day.'

Nestor, the elderly king of Pylos, tried to calm them down. He was like a father to them all. He begged Agamemnon not to take Achilles' girl. The commander-in-chief listened to the old man respectfully but stubbornly refused to back down.

Odysseus had listened in horror and disbelief. If Nestor with all his eloquence had failed, what could he say or do. He went and got the priest's daughter from Agamemnon's quarters and took her back to her father. The Greeks offered sacrifices and the plague came to an end. The emergency was over but they had lost the support of their greatest warrior and made a formidable enemy – the god Apollo.

Achilles cried out for vengeance and his mother, the nymph Thetis, came out of the sea to comfort him.

Achilles slumped on the sea shore and cried out to his mother for vengeance. In her home deep beneath the waves, the nymph Thetis heard his voice and came up to console him. Achilles poured out his sorrows and she promised to seek the help of Zeus, the king of the gods.

Thetis found the great god sitting alone on the highest peak of Mount Olympus. The other gods were a little further down the mountain where they all had their palaces. Zeus listened sympathetically as Thetis told him how disgracefully her son had been treated, but the king of the gods was worried. Several of the gods had already taken sides in the war and he wanted

to remain neutral. Naturally enough, Aphrodite was supporting Paris and the Trojans. Hera and Athena had never forgiven Paris and supported the Greeks. Now Apollo had joined the Trojan side. Soon the war would spread to heaven itself.

That night, whilst the other gods slept peacefully, Zeus tossed and turned wondering how he could avenge Achilles. He decided to convince Agamemnon that Troy would fall if he made an all-out attack. Then, when the Greeks had committed all their forces he would let the Trojans overwhelm them. Agamemon would have to grovel before Achilles or see his army wiped out. The king of the gods was pleased – it was an excellent plan. He called a False Dream and explained what he wanted.

Thetis threw herself at Zeus' feet and begged the king of the Gods to help her son. But Zeus was worried. Already the other gods and goddesses had taken sides and were plotting together.

Ares

Poseidon

Aphrodite

Apollo

Athena

Hera

11

Empires in Chaos

A Golden Age

The legend of Odysseus is based on the two earliest pieces of European literature, the Iliad and the Odyssey. These two epic poems are believed to have been composed by the Greek poet Homer some time in the 8th century BC. They tell of a Golden Age long before the poet's time and of the heroes who fought in the legendary Trojan war.

Few people believed that there was any truth in these legends until 100 years ago when the amateur archaeologist Heinrich Schliemann astonished the world by digging up the ruins of Troy.

The Mycenaeans

Since the discovery of Troy many of the legendary sites of Greece, including Mycenae, have been unearthed. This has opened up an entirely new era of history and proved that there was indeed a great civilization in Greece 1,000 years before the time of Plato. Homer called these early people Achaeans or Danaans. Today we call them Mycenaeans. They spoke a dialect of ancient Greek and used a simple type of picture writing now known as Linear B.

RIGHT: a late Mycenaean sceptre from Kourion-Kaloriziki in Cyprus.
BELOW: an earlier gold Mycenaean mask from one of the shaft graves at Mycenae once thought to be Agamemnon's

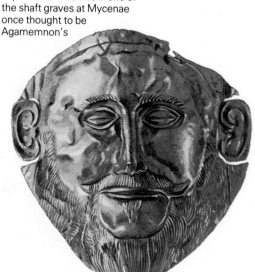

A balance of power

The Mycenaeans were a sea-faring people. Their ships traded all over the eastern Mediterranean. They had settlements in Cyprus and on the coast of Syria.

The Mycenaean expansion eastwards was checked by two peoples, the Hittites who occupied much of modern Turkey, and the Egyptians. These three peoples kept a balance of power.

The balance is shattered

About 1285BC the Hittites and Egyptians went to war. A great chariot battle was fought at Kadesh in Syria which was indecisive, but it broke the strength of both states. Egypt survived, but the Hittite empire collapsed within a century, bringing anarchy to the eastern Mediterranean.

A mystery

The collapse of the Hittites is a mystery. Excavations at Hattusa, the Hittite capital, show that it was massively fortified — yet it was sacked. Only an enemy with advanced technical skills could have breached its defences. No such enemy existed.

The great catastrophe

About the same time, catastrophe struck Greece too. Most of the citadels were overthrown. Mycenae, Tiryns and Pylos were all burned around 1200BC. Ugarit in Syria, Tarsus in southern Turkey, and Enkomi in Cyprus were all sacked around this time — and so was Troy. Was this coincidence or were these events connected?

The Sea Peoples

In 1186BC a vast horde of invaders descended on Egypt. They came by land and sea. A desperate battle was fought in the Nile delta and the Egyptians just managed to drive them out.

Could these invaders have overthrown the Hittite empire and burned the Mycenaean citadels? Some of the places mentioned above may have been destroyed by them but it seems far more likely that these invasions were the result, and not the cause, of the collapse of Hittite and Mycenaean power.

No simple answer

History is seldom simple. Events usually have many causes. Later Greeks believed that Zeus started the Trojan war to reduce the world's population. Could there be a germ of truth in this? Over-population coupled with climatic change and famine could have led to the overthrow of central authority. The rise of piracy on both land and sea would automatically follow the breakdown of law and order. The Trojan war probably took place in the midst of these upheavals. The piratical raids made by the Greeks on the surrounding lands fits this pattern well.

The Mycenaeans never really recovered. By the end of the 12th century BC Greece had sunk into a dark age that lasted for more than 400 years.

LEFT: a Mycenaean clay tablet from Crete. Mycenaean writing is known as Linear B. Many of these tablets appear to give lists of goods.

RIGHT: a sculpture from Thebes in Egypt showing the battle of Kadesh c1285BC.

FAR RIGHT: a sculpture from the temple at Medinet Habu in Egypt showing the defeat of the people who tried to invade Egypt by land in 1186BC.

BELOW: map of the eastern Mediterranean. The red spots show the main Mycenaean settlements in the 13th century BC.

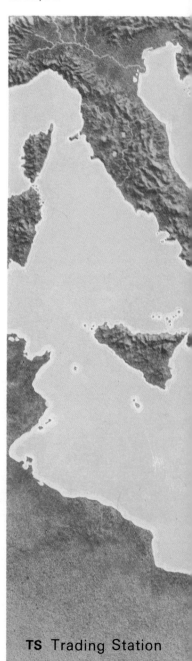

TS Trading Station

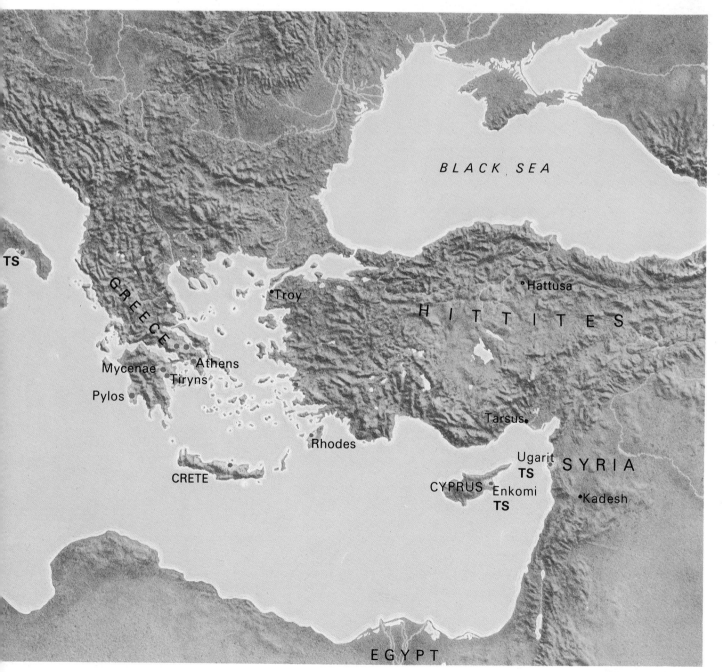

BLACK SEA

TS

GREECE

Troy

HITTITES

•Hattusa

Mycenae   Athens
       Tiryns
Pylos

Rhodes

Tarsus•

CRETE

Ugarit
TS

SYRIA

CYPRUS Enkomi
        TS

•Kadesh

EGYPT

Agamemnon's Citadel
at Mycenae

The centre of power

The citadel at Mycenae was built on a hillock overlooking the Plain of Argos. Traces of at least four major roads have been found leading to the citadel identifying it as the most important centre in the area and supporting Homer's claim that it was the foremost kingdom in Greece.

The citadel is crowned by a palace with a great columned hall known as a megaron (**A** on the picture opposite). The temples (**B,C**) and the graves of the early kings (**D**) are further down the slope.

The cyclopean walls

The citadel is surrounded by massive walls between 5.5 and 7.5 metres thick. Some of the stones are so huge that later Greeks believed that they must have been built by Cyclopses. (page 54). At one point the walls are still 8.25m high and may originally have been as much as 12m high.

The main gate (**E**) is known as the Lion Gate from the two lions carved above the lintel. It was defended by a bastion (**F**) from which missiles could be hurled at the unshielded side of any attackers. There is a similar gate in the north wall (**G**). About the time of the Trojan war the north-east corner (**H**) was extended to cover the water supply which was reached through a tunnel under the wall.

ABOVE: the Lion Gate at Mycenae, the main entrance to the citadel. It was built in the middle of the 13th century BC just before the Trojan war. The lintel is 4.5m long and weighs about 18 tons.

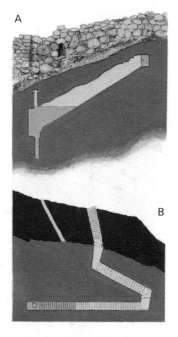

ABOVE: **A**: section of the stepped tunnel leading to the secret water supply just outside the walls of the citadel. The hole in the wall is a sally port through which surprise attacks could be launched on the enemy.
B: Plan of the tunnel.

A reconstruction of Mycenae as it must have looked at the time of the Trojan war.
A megaron. **B,C** temples.
D Grave circle. **E** Lion Gate.
F bastion. **G** north-east gate.
H north-east extension.

Ships

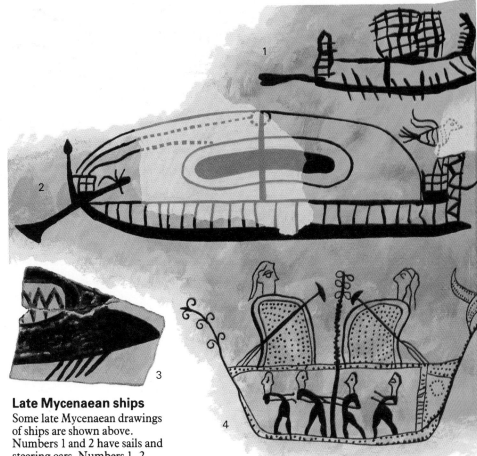

The ships from Thera

Very little is known about late Mycenaean ships. There are some crude vase paintings but these only show their basic form.

However, there is a detailed painting from the Aegean island of Thera which shows a procession of ships. This was painted some 300 years before the Trojan war but it may throw some light on the later ships.

At this time most ships were rowed, but these (number 6 below) are being paddled like canoes. A small boat (number 5) from the same fresco proves that these people knew how to row. A square sail appears to be stowed above the passengers. The loops at the top of the mast show how it was raised. The ship was steered with a large oar.

Unsolved problems

This picture unfortunately raises many problems. There appears to be a ram at the rear of the ship, but this has been hotly disputed.

If it is a ram then the ship must be going backwards. Ships with rams had to be beached backwards and it is possible that this is what this ship is doing. On the other hand it may show a traditional ceremony in which the ships were used abnormally.

Late Mycenaean ships

Some late Mycenaean drawings of ships are shown above. Numbers 1 and 2 have sails and steering oars. Numbers 1, 2 and 3 have a ram or projection at the front. Number 4 has a mast with loops similar to the Thera Ship and the men below the deck appear, if anything, to be rowing and not paddling. Number 2 has a raised platform at either end with railings. The upright lines along the length of this ship are probably an attempt to show the benches and should not be interpreted as a raised deck.

ABOVE: four crude paintings of ships from late Mycenaean vases. The lighter areas have been restored.

Two of the boats shown on ship fresco from Thera. The island was destroyed by a volcanic explosion and buried ashes c1500BC.

6

Sea Peoples

at naval battle between
ptians and the Sea
in 1186BC is illustrated
alls of the Egyptian
t Medinet Habu. The
les' ships have two
in common with late
ean vessels. They have
latforms at the front
k, and the birds' heads
end may have some
ion with what appear to
on numbers 2 and 4

r's ships

ps described by Homer
bably those of his own
50BC. There are two
pes, fast light ships with
, and heavier warships
oars. These ships were
not paddled. Leather
or the oars are often
ned. They had sails but
ere only used when the
as in the right direction.
tones were used for
. Several dating from
cenaean era have been

ships

's ships are most often
ed as black, probably
their keels were tarred.
the water level they
e any colour. Odysseus'
ad blue prows.

LEFT: three stone anchors from the Mycenaean period. The one at the top had two stakes through it to stop it dragging along the sea bed. The one at the bottom left is decorated in the form of an octopus.

ABOVE: a sculpture from the temple at Medinet Habu in Egypt showing a Sea Peoples' vessel. It has a raised platform at either end and the front and rear posts are decorated with birds' heads.

BELOW: an imaginative reconstruction of one of Odysseus' ships. These held fifty men and probably had fifty oars. It is shown with both sails and oars but these would not be used at the same time.

2

DAYS OF DEATH

The duel

As dawn tinted the eastern sky with crimson, Agamemnon rose from his bed. He called a council of the kings and told them of a dream he had had. He assured them that at last Troy would fall. The kings, convinced that his dream was divinely inspired, agreed to act on it. They told their men to breakfast and prepare for battle. Each man sacrificed to his favourite god and prayed for help in the coming fight. Odysseus, as always, made his offering to Athena the goddess of wisdom, whilst Agamemnon sacrificed an ox to Zeus on behalf of the whole army.

The Trojans knew that Achilles had withdrawn, and their spirits soared. They streamed out of the city and down onto the plain. For the first time since the Greeks had arrived, nine long years ago, they were prepared to fight in the open. A vast horde of friends and allies had swollen their numbers, and now they felt themselves more than a match for the Greeks. The order was given and with much shouting the Trojans began to advance across the plain in a great cloud of dust.

Paris was carried away by the excitement. In a fleeting moment of courage he dashed out in front of the Trojan army and challenged any Greek champion to single combat. Achilles' absence had gone to his head and he had forgotten that there were other Greek heroes. But when Menelaus, his armour flashing in the morning sun, rushed forward to accept the challenge Paris quickly disappeared into his own lines. As he slunk away he found his path blocked by Hector.

'You pathetic boy,' Hector jeered at him. 'You're great with the women but what a gutless coward you really are. You steal a man's wife and then you haven't even the courage to face the consequences. We should have stoned you to death years ago for all the evil you have brought on us.'

His brother's words cut deeply and Paris sullenly agreed to fight. Hector stepped out into the space between the two armies and held back the Trojan line. Agamemnon did the same and ordered his archers to stop shooting. As soon as his voice could be heard Hector repeated Paris' challenge. He proposed that the whole war should be decided by the duel, the winner taking Helen and her treasure.

Both sides held their breath waiting for Menelaus' reply. When he accepted they raised a great cheer. At last they saw an end to the fighting. A truce was agreed and sealed with sacrifices. There could be no way back now.

Hector and Odysseus marked out the ground whilst Paris and Menelaus prepared themselves. The old men, women and children of Troy were crowding onto the battlements to watch. Priam and Helen had climbed to the top of the great tower overlooking the Scaean gate. Helen knew that within a few minutes her fate would be decided.

Each contestant was given a spear and sword on stepping into the arena. They warily circled about, brandishing their weapons and glaring at each other. Lots had been cast and Paris had won the right to strike first. He continued to circle the Greek searching for an opening in his defence. Menelaus, knees slightly bent, ready to dart either to left or right, eyed his opponent cautiously over the top of his shield.

Suddenly Paris leapt in and hurled his spear. Menelaus jumped sideways, and deflected the spear with his shield, making it fall harmlessly to the ground. It was now Menelaus' turn. He sensed that Paris was quivering with fear behind his great shield. The Greek dashed sideways and flung his spear hoping to get round Paris' guard. Paris reacted just in time and caught the full force of the weapon in the centre of his shield. It ripped through the hide and Paris gasped when he saw the point appear on the inside. He twisted his body avoiding death by a hair's breadth. The spear glanced along the side of his cuirass ripping into the metal and tearing the tunic.

Before Paris could recover Menelaus was on him, sword in hand. Driven on by years of pent up anger he struck Paris such a blow on the helmet that his sword shattered into several pieces. Menelaus cursed Zeus for his bad luck and grabbed the crest of Paris' helmet. The Trojan, who had been stunned by the sword blow, was now wrenched off his feet. Menelaus swung him round by his crest and began to drag him off to the Greek lines. Paris choked as his helmet strap tightened round his throat. He struggled desperately but his face was beginning to turn blue.

Menelaus grabbed the crest of Paris' helmet, wrenched him off his feet and began to drag him towards the Greek lines.

Then Aphrodite, seeing what was happening, darted in and cut the strap. In anger and frustration Menelaus hurled the helmet into his own lines. He had no weapons and was at Paris' mercy. This was Paris' great chance. But he had had enough and Aphrodite helped him flee back to his own lines.

A battle with the gods

Hera and Athena, furious at Aphrodite's interference, were even more determined to have their revenge. They went to Zeus and he agreed that the war must go on.

Menelaus was still stomping up and down the lines shouting for Paris, when the Trojan archer Pandarus, egged on by the two goddesses, took a pot shot at him. The arrow caused only a minor wound but the truce was broken. Soon spears were flying back and forth and men began to fall on either side. The battle was on.

Diomedes, the king of Argos, stormed into the fray, bellowing his war cry and killing all who opposed him. But Pandarus the archer had seen him. Diomedes staggered backwards. He shouted to his charioteer for help. Pandarus' arrow had pierced the hero's shoulder guard and the barbed point was sticking out of his back. The charioteer broke off the feathered flight and pulled the shaft of the arrow through. Blood spurted from the wound but Athena was quick to quench the flow and give Diomedes the strength to fight on.

Back into the throng he charged, searching angrily for Pandarus. The archer had exchanged his bow for a spear and was now bearing down on Diomedes in a chariot. The Trojan hurled his spear and its point tore through Diomedes' shield and hit his cuirass. But Pandarus' shout of triumph was cut short as Diomedes' huge spear struck him in the face and severed his tongue.

Aphrodite's son, Aeneas, who had been driving the chariot, jumped down determined to stop Diomedes stripping Pandarus' corpse. He stood astride the body like a lion guarding its prey and jabbed his spear at the Greek hero, keeping him back. Diomedes grabbed a huge, jagged piece of rock and hurled it at the Trojan. It caught him on the hip tearing through the flesh and smashing the bone. Aeneas sank to his knees with a groan but, before Diomedes could get to him, Aphrodite swooped down and carried off her wounded son.

Diomedes chased the goddess through the crowd lunging at her with his spear. She tried to avoid the thrust but the point caught her hand and screaming she dropped Aeneas. Diomedes shouted in triumph: 'You feeble goddess, keep to tempting women and leave war to men.'

He dashed in to seize the body but Apollo had now arrived on the scene. The god took over the defence of Aeneas concealing him in a dark blue cloud while Aphrodite ran off sobbing to her mother. Diomedes lunged even at Apollo. The god parried the blow but when the Greek returned to the attack he shouted a warning: 'Think, Diomedes, think. Do you believe that you are equal to the gods?'

Realizing that he had gone too far, Diomedes lowered his spear and withdrew.

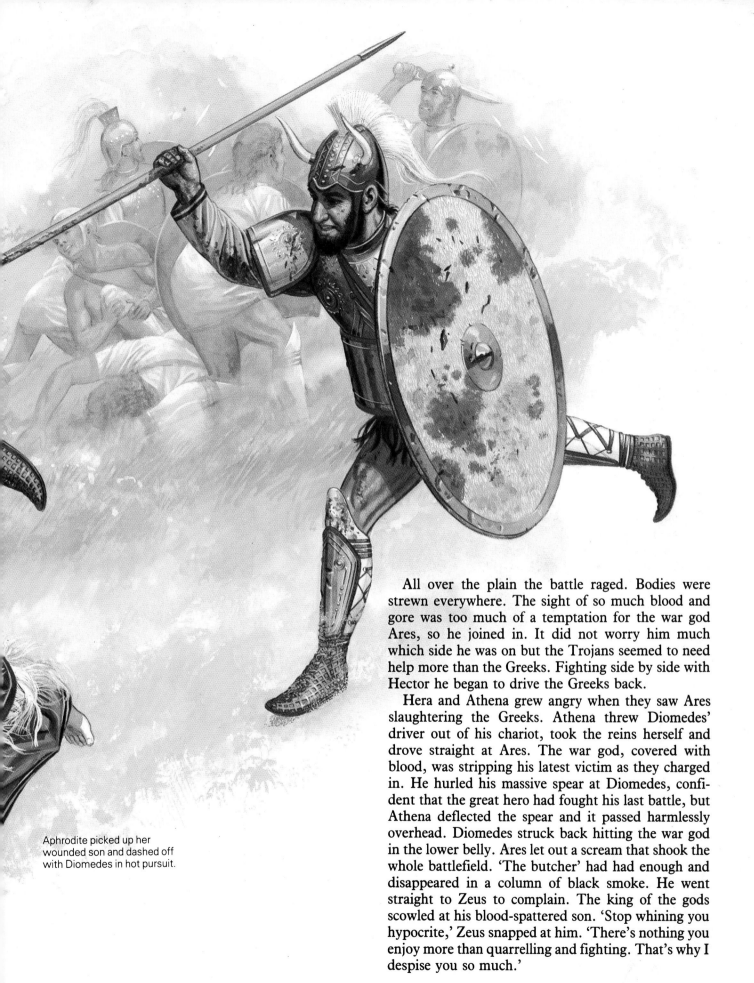

Aphrodite picked up her wounded son and dashed off with Diomedes in hot pursuit.

All over the plain the battle raged. Bodies were strewn everywhere. The sight of so much blood and gore was too much of a temptation for the war god Ares, so he joined in. It did not worry him much which side he was on but the Trojans seemed to need help more than the Greeks. Fighting side by side with Hector he began to drive the Greeks back.

Hera and Athena grew angry when they saw Ares slaughtering the Greeks. Athena threw Diomedes' driver out of his chariot, took the reins herself and drove straight at Ares. The war god, covered with blood, was stripping his latest victim as they charged in. He hurled his massive spear at Diomedes, confident that the great hero had fought his last battle, but Athena deflected the spear and it passed harmlessly overhead. Diomedes struck back hitting the war god in the lower belly. Ares let out a scream that shook the whole battlefield. 'The butcher' had had enough and disappeared in a column of black smoke. He went straight to Zeus to complain. The king of the gods scowled at his blood-spattered son. 'Stop whining you hypocrite,' Zeus snapped at him. 'There's nothing you enjoy more than quarrelling and fighting. That's why I despise you so much.'

Ajax and Hector

With Ares out of the fight the Greeks gradually gained the upper hand. The Trojans were now in danger of being overwhelmed. It was already late in the afternoon but Hector knew that his men could not hold out till darkness fell. There was only one thing he could do: when the Greeks drew back a little to catch their breath before launching their final attack, he stepped out between the lines and challenged them to put up a champion who would fight him in single combat.

The Greeks were horrified. Only Achilles could hope to beat Hector. Silently they cursed Agamemnon for what he had done. Already the great warrior's words were coming true. 'One day you will need me desperately . . .'

Honour prevented the Greeks refusing the challenge. They would have to select a champion by casting lots. The heroes each marked a piece of broken pottery and placed it in a helmet. While the army prayed old Nestor shook the helmet until one of the pieces jumped out. The lot was picked up and passed round. Odysseus stiffled a sigh of relief when he read Ajax's name on it.

The massive prince of Salamis willingly accepted the challenge and threw the lot at his feet. He was a giant of a man and carried a vast shield that seemed almost like a tower. It was made of seven layers of hide trimmed with bronze.

Everyone gasped when Ajax entered the arena. Even Hector was a little disconcerted when he saw the size of him. With a grim smile on his face Ajax walked right up to Hector and glared down at him defiantly.

'Hector,' he said, 'You thought you were going to have an easy victory. But now you will find out what sort of champions the Greeks have at their disposal when they can't count on Achilles. You've won the right to throw first, so start the fight.'

Hector shook his head.

'You don't frighten me, Ajax. What do you think I am, some feeble child or a woman who knows nothing about fighting. Be on your guard.' With this Hector flung his spear. It struck Ajax's shield but failed to pierce all the layers of hide. The Greek struck back with a colossal throw. His spear burst through Hector's shield but the Trojan managed to avoid the point.

They retrieved their spears and circled each other looking for an opening. Hector threw his spear with all his might. It struck Ajax's shield but only succeeded in bending the point of the spear. Ajax leapt forward

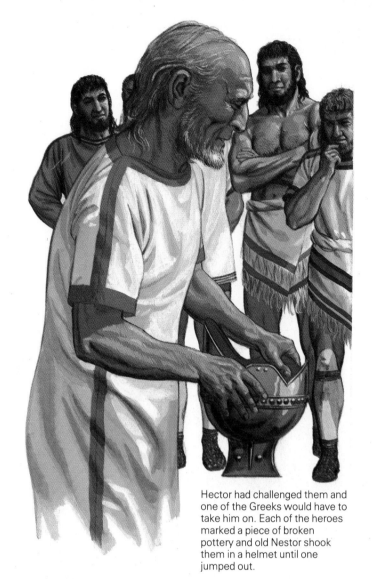

Hector had challenged them and one of the Greeks would have to take him on. Each of the heroes marked a piece of broken pottery and old Nestor shook them in a helmet until one jumped out.

his crest dancing above his helmet. Again his spear pierced Hector's shield but this time the Trojan was unable to avoid the point. It gashed his neck and blood poured down onto his cuirass.

Hector sank to his knees and for a second Ajax thought he had got him. But the Trojan picked up a piece of jagged rock and flung it with all the strength he could muster. The rock hit the bronze boss in the centre of Ajax's shield and the sound rang out across the plain. This change of tactics suited Ajax. He picked up a massive boulder and sent it hurtling towards his opponent with such force that it crumpled Hector's shield and knocked him off his feet. But before Ajax could close in for the kill Hector was up on his feet again.

The two sides had watched the fight with mounting excitement. It seemed a pity that either of these two great champions should lose. The sun had begun to sink behind the hills casting long shadows across the plain and both sides agreed that the fight should be called off. The two champions accepted the decision, exchanged gifts and parted friends.

Ajax hurled the boulder with such force that it buckled Hector's shield and sent the Trojan hero crashing to the ground.

At first light the following morning Paris sent out a messenger with an offer to return Menelaus' treasure and pay compensation for the loss of Helen. Though the proposal was rejected a truce was agreed so that both sides could honour their dead. A huge pyre was erected in front of each camp on which the bodies were burned. The following day the Greeks erected a great mound over the burned out pyre and extended it to form a defensive rampart in front of the ships in case the Trojans tried to burn them. The earthen wall had gateways and wooden towers at intervals and was topped with a fence.

When it was finished the Greeks retired wearily to their huts. But they slept uneasily that night as Zeus thundered ominously above them.

Zeus intervenes

Things had not quite worked out as Zeus had planned. The following morning he called all the gods together and gave them a stern warning: 'Any god that I catch interfering and helping either the Greeks or the Trojans will get a good thrashing and will be expelled from Olympus.'

The other gods, terrified of Zeus, sullenly agreed. Only Athena had the courage to speak up. 'Surely we can give them advice', she insisted

Zeus relented a little but demanded that they do no more than that.

The king of the gods took up his position on Mount Ida, to the south of Troy, where he could watch the two armies fighting it out on the plain below. At midday he held up his golden scales and placed the sentence of death on either side. The Greek side tipped down and their fate was sealed. The great god hurled a flash of lightning into their ranks. The Greeks turned white with terror, the line broke and they dashed for the shelter of the camp.

One of Nestor's horses had been struck by an arrow and he was left stranded on the battlefield. Hector noticed the old man and charged across the plain towards him. Death was staring Nestor in the face. But Diomedes had seen him too; he whipped his thoroughbreds, dashed along the line and, pulling the old man aboard, turned to meet Hector's attack. Nestor took over the reins whilst Diomedes hurled his spear at the approaching Trojan. The spear missed Hector but hit his driver. The Trojan's horses shied and the Greeks charged in for the kill.

This was not part of Zeus' plan. With a roar the angry god launched a blazing thunderbolt which crashed in front of Diomedes' horses. The stench of burning sulphur struck terror into the animals and Nestor had to struggle to keep control of them. He managed to turn the chariot and dash for the safety of the camp.

The Greek heroes tried to make a stand at the ditch in front of the rampart but when Hector arrived they were driven back into the camp with appalling losses. Only the gradual onset of night saved them from an even greater catastrophe.

Agamemnon knew by now that his vision had been false. A meeting of the kings was called and old Nestor got right to the heart of the matter. 'Agamemnon, you are a good king,' he said. 'But you cannot control your temper. You know that you were wrong to humiliate Achilles. Give him back the girl and make amends.'

The battle was not going as Zeus had planned. When he saw Nestor and Diomedes bearing down on Hector the angry god hurled a thunderbolt at them.

The commander-in-chief had lost all his bluster and arrogance. He admitted that he had been wrong and agreed to hand over the girl with massive compensation for the insults Achilles had suffered.

Odysseus and Ajax walked along the beach to Achilles' hut and put Agamemnon's offer to the great warrior. Achilles received them cordially for they were both his friends but he stood firm by his decision not to fight.

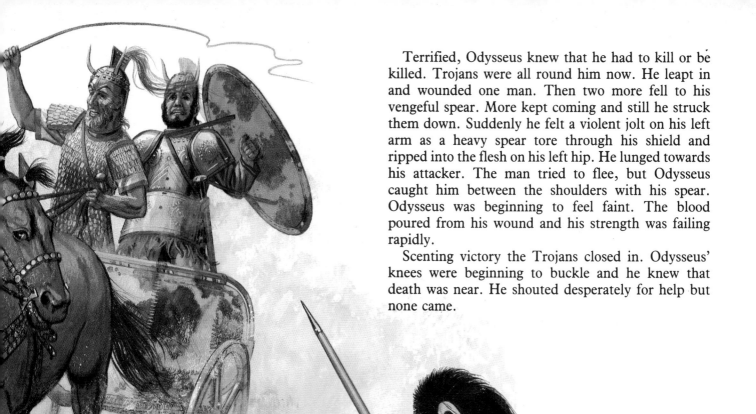

Terrified, Odysseus knew that he had to kill or be killed. Trojans were all round him now. He leapt in and wounded one man. Then two more fell to his vengeful spear. More kept coming and still he struck them down. Suddenly he felt a violent jolt on his left arm as a heavy spear tore through his shield and ripped into the flesh on his left hip. He lunged towards his attacker. The man tried to flee, but Odysseus caught him between the shoulders with his spear. Odysseus was beginning to feel faint. The blood poured from his wound and his strength was failing rapidly.

Scenting victory the Trojans closed in. Odysseus' knees were beginning to buckle and he knew that death was near. He shouted desperately for help but none came.

The spear had ripped through his shield and caught him in the side. As the blood gushed from the wound Odysseus felt his legs becoming weak.

The next morning the Greeks summoned up sufficient confidence to leave the camp and advance into the plain. But their faltering courage was shattered when Agamemnon himself was wounded and had to be carried from the field. Once more the line broke. Only Odysseus held his ground; he shouted to Diomedes above the din of battle, begging his old friend to stand with him. Together they rushed yelling into the Trojan throng dealing death wherever they went.

Hector saw what was happening and forced his way towards them, followed by his companies of native Trojans. Diomedes and Odysseus watched him coming and their stomachs turned. As Hector charged in, Diomedes' spear struck him on the top of the helmet. The Trojan champion staggered and fell to his knees. But he managed to struggle to his feet and withdrew before Diomedes could reach him. But just as the Greeks were congratulating themselves disaster struck and an arrow caught Diomedes in the foot. Unable to fight on, the hero hobbled back to his chariot leaving Odysseus alone.

The battle for the ships

Odysseus cried for help again and again and at last someone heard him. In seconds Ajax and Menelaus were forcing a way through to him. Ajax charged into the Trojans and drove them back giving Menelaus the chance to drag Odysseus into his chariot.

Ajax had changed positions with Odysseus and now found himself in the same hopeless predicament. The time for heroics had passed. As soon as he could see that Odysseus was safe, he slung his great shield round to cover his back and made a hasty retreat. Every now and then he turned to beat off his pursuers until finally he caught up with the rest of the retreating army.

Seeing the Greeks crowding back into their camp, the Trojans raised a mighty roar, stormed across the ditch and started to clamber up the rampart. The wind was howling across the plain blowing clouds of dust into the faces of the Greeks as they tried desperately to hold off the Trojans. The attackers tried to undermine the wooden towers and struggled to pull down the palisade. Finally a whole section of the breastwork gave way. With courage bordering on fanatacism Ajax leapt into the breach and held the Trojans back. With Agamemnon, Diomedes and Odysseus wounded the huge prince of Salamis had assumed command. But his heroism was to no avail. For even as he drove the Trojans from the wall Hector smashed down one of the gates and before the Greeks realized what was happening the Trojans were flooding into the camp.

Ajax yelled encouragement to his comrades but there was no holding the Trojans. Hour after hour the battle raged, and slowly but surely the Greeks were forced ever further back. The scene of death and destruction was the worst of the whole war.

Zeus lost interest now that the Trojans had broken into the Greek camp and Achilles had been avenged. But the sea god Poseidon was filled with pity for the Greeks. He had climbed to the lofty summit of the island of Samothrace and had been watching the battle from there. When he noticed that Zeus was not paying attention, he slipped into the Greek camp and took command. Encouraged by the presence of the sea god the Greeks now counter-attacked. Ajax hurled a massive rock at Hector and knocked him off his feet but before the Greeks could get at him, the Trojans closed ranks around him and he was carried back to his chariot. The Trojans lost heart without their leader and were soon driven back across the rampart and over the ditch.

Suddenly Zeus noticed what was happening and angrily ordered Poseidon to get back to the sea where he belonged. He then despatched Apollo to cure Hector and put the fear of the gods into the Greeks.

With Hector restored the tide of battle turned once more. The Greeks were thrown back in disorder, the rampart was breached and the Trojans poured into the camp again. Step by step the Greeks were driven down the beach until they were fighting amongst the ships whilst overhead Zeus thundered his applause.

Ajax fought like a lion but Hector finally cornered him near his ships. The Greek hero struggled desperately but the pressure was too great. He leapt up onto the stern of one of his ships and fought from there, thrusting out at the Trojans with a long bronze-pointed pole normally used for sea battles. Again and again Hector tried to dislodge him so that he could set fire to the ship but, though showered with arrows and javelins, Ajax refused to budge and the bodies began to pile up around the keel of the ship.

As more and more Trojans moved in to the attack Ajax's position became ever more desperate. Jumping from ship to ship he frantically tried to ward off the attackers. Though he fought with super-human courage he was eventually driven back from the stern. He fought on from the bridge lunging at the Trojans with the long pole until Hector slashed the point off it. Was it all over? Flames began to lap the tarred hulls and billows of smoke darkened the sky.

Ajax leapt up onto the stern of one of his ships. Using a long spiked pole he drove the Trojans back again and again. But finally he was overwhelmed and driven from his position. It seemed that nothing could save the Greeks now.

The Warrior: Helmets

5 Figures shown on the Warrior Vase from Mycenae c1200BC. These are the best representations of warriors from the Trojan war period. They wear horned helmets, body armour, and leg guards, and they carry moon shaped shields.

The Homeric warrior

Homer's warriors seem to be a jumble of Mycenaean traditions padded out with details from the poet's own day (c750BC). The hero rides into battle in a chariot but fights on foot. He is usually armed with two heavy throwing spears and a sword. He wears body armour, helmet and leg guards. He also has a large round shield hanging from a strap around his neck which can be swung round to protect his back.

Mycenaean paintings

Many pictures of Mycenaean warriors have been found. Most wear helmets and leg guards but no body armour. The Sea Peoples (below, numbers 3 and 4) have body armour, helmets and large round shilds with a central handgrip.

The most interesting representation of late Mycenaean warriors comes from Mycenae itself. The Warrior Vase (number 5) was one of the first Mycenaean artefacts found. It shows warriors fully armed with helmet, body armour, leg guards and shields.

6 A bronze helmet from Tiryns c1050BC. It has embossed decoration similar to helmets from central Europe. Compare number 13.

7 A bronze helmet from Knossos in Crete c1400BC. The cheek pieces were probably stitched to the helmet. The top knot was pierced to hold a crest. This is a very common central European type of helmet.

1 A fragmentary wall painting from Tiryns showing a warrior or huntsman with two spears.

2 A fragmentary wall painting from Pylos showing a warrior with a boar's tusk helmet, leg guards and short thrusting sword.

3 One of the Sea Peoples from Medinet Habu in Egypt. He has a horned helmet and a large round shield with a central handgrip.

4 Another of the Sea Peoples from Medinet Habu in Egypt. He has a so-called 'feather' helmet, a cuirass with shoulder guards and a long thrusting sword.

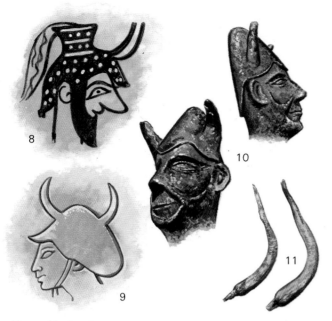

Boar's tusk helmets

In the Iliad Homer describes a helmet worn by Odysseus as being unique: "a helmet wrought of hide, with many a tight stretched thong was it made stiff within". On the outside boars' tusks were "set thick on this side and that". Far from being unique this is the commonest form of helmet shown in Mycenaean art. The possible reconstruction of such a helmet is shown below (number 20). The hide thongs probably criss-crossed over the crown making it thicker on top where the full force of a blow would be felt. Some helmets appear to have the ends of the thongs hanging down at the back to form a flexible neck guard as shown here. The inside of the helmet was lined with felt.

'Feather Helmets'

The so-called 'feather' helmets worn by the Sea Peoples (numbers 15 and 16) may be made in much the same way as the boar's tusk helmets but with the thongs turned up at the ends and held in place with a band possibly made of bronze.

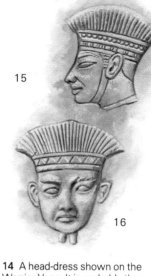

14 A head-dress shown on the Warrior Vase. It is probably the same as those shown on the Egyptian sculptures (15 and 16) These show the so-called 'feather' helmets.

17, 18 Paintings of boar's tusk helmets from Pylos.

19 Parts of a boar's tusk helmet from Mycenae.

20 A reconstruction of a boar's tusk helmet.

Horned helmets

8 A horned helmet shown on the Warrior Vase from Mycenae. The white lines and dots probably represent embossing.

9 A Sea People's horned helmet from the temple at Medinet Habu in Egypt.

10 Two views of the head of the 12th century 'Ingot god' from Enkomi in Cyprus.

11 Horns from Dendra in Greece.

12 A horned helmet on a statue from Ugarit in Syria.

13 An embossed bronze helmet from Pass Lueg in Austria – probably c1300BC. Similar decoration was used in Greece from the 13th century BC. This type of helmet was made of two pieces riveted together. The Warrior Vase helmets (5 and 8) were also probably made in this way.

Mycenaean Helmets

Only two Greek helmets of this period have been found. One from Crete (number 7 on the left) was made some 200 years before the Trojan war. The other (number 6) found at Tiryns was made about 150 years after the war.

The Tiryns helmet is decorated with embossed patterns – a style originating in central Europe. Fragments of embossed armour have been found in late Mycenaean graves showing that this style of decoration was in use at the time of the Trojan war.

Horned helmets

Most of the figures on the Warrior Vase wear horned helmets. These were common in the eastern Mediterranean at this time. The Warrior Vase helmets have a projection over the top of the nose. This feature can be seen on the examples shown in the box above. The white spots shown on the Warrior Vase helmets probably represent embossed decoration.

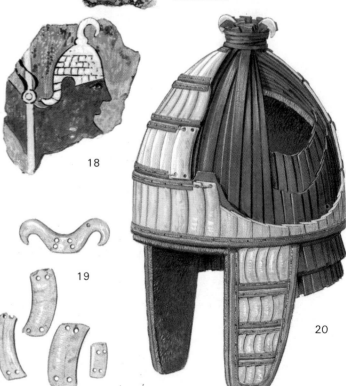

The Warrior: Body Armour and Weapons

Scale armour

Virtually no body armour from the late Mycenaean period has survived. Scales were found at Mycenae and Troy (right numbers 2 and 3). This, the oldest form of armour, was used widely. A scale cuirass is shown on an Egyptian wall painting (right number 1). The neck guard on this cuirass is similar to the one from the Dendra armour (below). Both date from the 15th century BC.

The Dendra armour

The earliest example of a beaten bronze cuirass was found at Dendra in southern Greece. It is part of the Dendra panoply, consisting of 15 separate pieces joined together with thongs.

LEFT: a reconstruction of the Dendra warrior.

BELOW: an exploded drawing of the Dendra armour.
A, B Two-part cuirass hinged on left side. C Inside and outside of hinge. D Loop fastening on right side. E, E Shoulder guards. F, F Upper arm guards. G Neck guard. H, H Plates covering

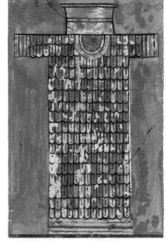

abdomen and upper legs. X, Y Suspension of front plates.

ABOVE: 1 Painting of a scale cuirass from Thebes in Egypt. 2 and 3 Bronze scales from Mycenae and Troy. Scale 1:3.

ABOVE: Bronze embossed cuirass from Switzerland.
RIGHT: **4** Linear B symbol for a cuirass.
5 Fragments of a late Mycenaean embossed cuirass from Kallithea in Greece.
6 Fragments of two embossed cuirasses from Czechoslovakia.
7 Body armour shown on the Warrior Vase from Mycenae.

BELOW: reconstructions of hacking and slashing swords. Homer claims that these weapons could sever an arm.

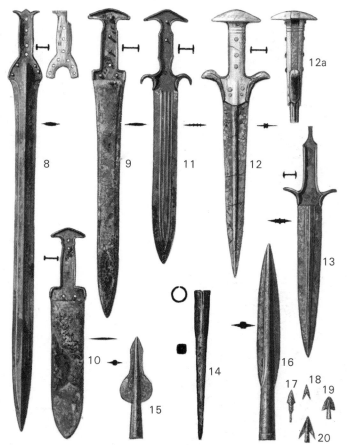

BELOW RIGHT: bronze weapons of the Trojan War era. Scale 1:6.
8–13 Swords. **14** Spear butt.
15–16 Spear heads.
17–20 Arrow heads.

8,11,14 and **17–19** are from Greece
9–12 From Crete
13,15 From Turkey
20 From Troy

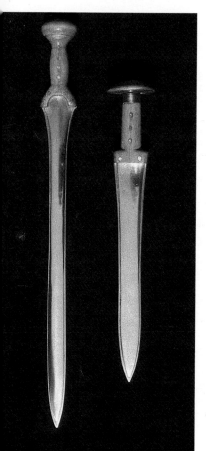

Armour in central Europe

Beaten bronze cuirasses were being made in central Europe in late Mycenaean times (left number 6). These fragments from two separate cuirasses are embossed like the helmets on the previous page.

Embossed cuirasses of a later date have been found in Switzerland. These were rivetted together on the left side but the right side was joined with a loop in the same way as the Dendra cuirass. This similarity implies that the two types had a common origin and that they remained in use throughout this period. But were they in use in Greece?

Linear B symbols

Although no late Mycenaean cuirass has been found, the 13th century BC Linear B symbol for armour appears often. These symbols (left number 4) bear a remarkable resemblance to the Dendra armour and suggest that the type was still in use. Therefore we should look at the late Mycenaean representations of armour with the Dendra panoply and the central European cuirasses in mind.

The Warrior Vase

Several figures on the Warrior Vase appear to be wearing body armour. The one on the left (number 7) seems to have an embossed cuirass with a plate hanging below it. Pieces of embossed bronze (number 5) were found in a warrior's grave at Kallithea in Greece. These could well be from a central European type of cuirass.

It is impossible to interpret the ladder patterns on either side of the cuirass shown on the Warrior Vase. The three lines on the right arm could mark the lower edge of a shoulder guard. There can be little doubt that shoulder guards are shown on the Sea Peoples' sculpture (page 29, number 8).

Spears

The Mycenaean warrior was a spearman. He only used his sword if his spear was lost or broken. Most of Homer's warriors prefer throwing stones to using their swords. Leaf-shaped spear heads (number 16) were common in the late Mycenaean period. Number 15 is probably of central European origin.

Mycenaean swords

Earlier Mycenaean swords were long pointed weapons designed for thrusting and not cutting. By the 13th century BC these had been replaced by much shorter weapons. Some were still designed for thrusting (number 12), but others were intended for chopping or hacking (numbers 9 and 11).

A new weapon

A new weapon had come to Greece which was to change the face of battle. It was a long slashing weapon (number 8) which originated in central Europe. Some examples are more than 80cm long. It was probably the most successful sword ever designed. Its iron successor was used by both Greeks and Romans until the 3rd century BC.

Arrows

The bow is discussed on page 75. Homer's heroes looked upon it as a cowardly weapon and most refused to use it. Many arrow heads have been found, most are no more than flat dart-shaped pieces of bronze (number 18) which were tied into a slot in the shaft.

The Warrior: Other Armour, Shields and Chariots

Arm and leg guards
The Dendra warrior had both leg and lower arm guards. The arm guard is unique but leg guards, probably made of linen, are often shown in late Mycenaean art. A few bronze examples have been found. These covered only the shins and may have been worn over linen ones.

Shields
In the Iliad, shields are usually described as round and very large. Agamemnon's shield can shelter a man on either side. Round shields are seldom seen in Mycenaean art but all the Sea Peoples use them (page 17 top, page 28 number 3), and they are common in central Europe. Homer's description could possibly also apply to shields with curved rims such as those on the Warrior Vase (page 28 number 5).

BELOW: **6** The central rib of the Lion Hunt dagger from Mycenae c1550BC. It shows figure-eight and tower shields complete with neck straps.
7 A figure-eight shield from the 'Battle of Kadesh' relief.

Ajax and Hector
In the dual between Ajax and Hector (page 23) both contestants used huge body shields. Homer compares Ajax's shield to a tower and as Hector walked off after the duel Homer says "the dark leather of his bossed shield tapped him on the ankles and neck". It has been argued that this was because Hector's shield had been knocked out of shape but this can hardly have had much effect on it length.

Body shields
Two forms of body shield were used in earlier Mycenaean times: the figure-eight and the tower type. Both forms are shown on the Lion Hunt dagger (below number 6). These shields disappear from Mycenaean art about 1400BC. Historians have concluded that Ajax and possibly Hector too came from an earlier legend that has been incorporated into the Iliad. However, it is possible that in some places these huge shields were still used.

The figure-eight shield
Shields clearly derived from the figure-eight type are common in Athenian art of the 8th century BC (number 9 below). Similar shields were used by the Hittites in the 13th century BC. A fragment of a painting from Pylos (number 8) shows a man holding what appears to be a figure-eight shield. This is not a round shield as the handgrip cannot be in the centre.

Bossed shields
Homer's shields were made of several layers of hide probably sewn to a wicker frame. They had bosses and were edged with bronze.
The remains of a bossed shield were found at Kaloriziki in Cyprus (below number 10). It is very small, scarcely 49cm wide. It has a large central boss with smaller ones on either side and a thin bronze rim. Unfortunately only part of the shield has survived, and it is impossible to be sure of its original shape, but at least it tells us what bosses were like and how a shield was edged.

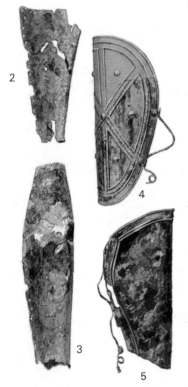

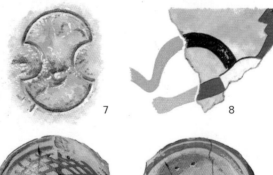

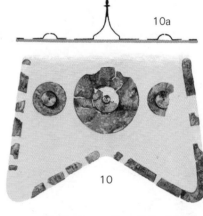

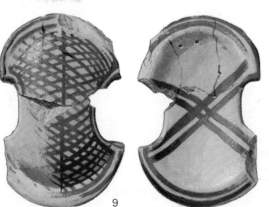

1 A fresco showing linen greaves held on with straps, from the palace at Pylos.
2 Bronze lower arm guard from the Warrior grave at Dendra.
3 Bronze greave from the Warrior grave at Dendra.
4 Bronze shin guard from Kallithea in Greece.
5 Bronze shin guard from Enkomi in Cyprus.

8 A fragment of a painting from Pylos showing what seems to be a figure-eight shield.
9 Front and back of a model shield from Athens c750BC.
10 Fragments of a bossed shield from Kaloriziki, Cyprus.
10a Section of the shield.

Chariots – a taxi service?

The chariots in the Iliad were not used for massed charges but merely for carrying the heroes to the front line where they got down and fought on foot. It is difficult to believe that chariots were used in this way such a short time after the great chariot battle of Kadesh c1285BC (page 12).

Celtic chariots

In the 4th–3rd century BC the Italian Celts used chariots in this way. But this was at a time when the chariot had become obsolete in Italy. Was this the case at the time of the Trojan War?

The chariots of Knossos

An inventory found in the armoury at Knossos in Crete lists 340 chariot bodies and 1,000 pairs of wheels. These can hardly have been used just to get the nobility to the front line. The ratio of three sets of wheels to each body implies that they were intended for rougher service than this. They must have been used for fighting.

ABOVE: carving of a chariot on an ivory casket from the Mycenaean settlement at Enkomi in Cyprus.
BELOW: a Linear B symbol for a chariot. It probably shows its construction.

Pictorial evidence

No recognizable parts of Mycenaean chariots have been found. The surviving paintings are often too stylized or damaged to give more than a fleeting impression. The fresco from Pylos (left number 1) tells us only that they had four-spoked wheels. The painting from Hagia Triada in Crete (number 5), confirms four-spoked wheels and shows a hide covered body.

Horses and harnessing

The lid of an ivory casket from Enkomi in Cyprus shows a chariot from the Trojan War period. It is pulled by two horses wearing blankets and blinkers. The six-spoked wheels may be due to Egyptian influence.

A fragment of a painting from Knossos in Crete (number 3) shows part of the yoke and harnessing. Others show details of the upper yoke bar and the horse's mane gathered in bunches.

1 A late Mycenaean chariot from a wall painting at Pylos.
2 A bronze snaffle bit from Mycenae.
3 Fragment of a painting from Knossos in Crete showing part of the yoke and harnessing.
4 Fragment of a painting from Tiryns showing the junction of the upper yoke bar and the body.
5 A painting from Hagia Triada in Crete. It shows a hide covered chariot body.

Religion and Burial Rites

Homer's Gods

The Gods of the Iliad are just super men. They have all the passions and faults of men but are immortal. They were the patrons of particular qualities, skills and activities, much as St Christopher is the patron saint of travellers. Artemis was the goddess of hunting, Athena of wisdom and war, Aphrodite of love, etc. But over the centuries many of the gods appear to have changed their status.

A Volcano god

Hephaestus was originally a volcano god. His scope was widened to include fire in general and by Homer's time he was the patron of smiths who used fire to forge metal. His own workshop was believed to be under Mount Etna, the volcano in Sicily.

Father of Gods and men

Homer calls Zeus 'father of gods and men'. How he got this title is a mystery for he is neither. Uranus, his grandfather has a better claim to this title.

Some of the gods such as Aphrodite and Apollo were his children but Poseidon and Hades were his brothers. Most of the others were his cousins, (see chart below). Why should such a claim be made? Was it because Zeus was a usurper and had no right to be king of the gods?

Zeus, the weather god

Zeus was not king of the gods in Mycenaean times. He was only the weather god. In later times he still kept many of the characteristics of a weather god. He was called the 'Thunderer' and lived on mountains to control the weather.

The Great Mother

The chief Mycenaean deity was Artemis the later goddess of hunting. She was worshipped as the mother goddess and combined the qualities of Athena, Hera and other later goddesses. By Homer's time she had become a minor deity.

A religious revolution

During the dark age that followed the fall of Mycenae some religious revolution must have taken place which promoted Zeus, and relegated Artemis to a minor position.

Poseidon of Pylos

Many of the other gods such as Ares, Athena and Hera were known in Mycenaean times. Poseidon's name occurs several times on the Linear B tablets from Pylos. He seems to have been important in this area. It is significant that in the Iliad, Nestor the king of Pylos sacrificed 81 bulls to him.

Idols

Many idols have been found at Mycenaean sites. These are usually very crudely made. The beautiful ivory group on the right is a unique exception. The commonest forms in the 13th century BC were the tiny statuettes known as Phi and Psi figures from their resemblance to these two Greek letters (below, numbers 1 and 2). A group of grotesque figures (far right, number 6) were found in the 'Room with Platforms' at Mycenae (see right). These seem to be exceptional. More attractive idols were found in neighbouring buildings.

An ivory carving of two goddesses with a child from Mycenae. This is one of the master-pieces of Mycenaean art.

BELOW: a family tree of the gods mentioned in this book. Athena was said to have sprung fully armed from Zeus' head.

ABOVE: a sacrificial scene from Hagia Triada in Crete. A priestess with the bull for sacrifice is standing at an altar in front of a shrine.

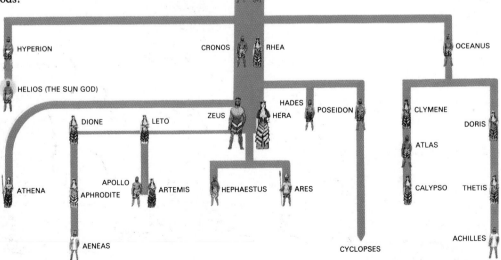

URANUS — GE
HYPERION — CRONOS — RHEA — OCEANUS
HELIOS (THE SUN GOD)
DIONE — LETO — ZEUS — HADES — POSEIDON — HERA — CLYMENE — DORIS
ATLAS
ATHENA — APOLLO APHRODITE — ARTEMIS — HEPHAESTUS — ARES — CALYPSO — THETIS
AENEAS — CYCLOPSES — ACHILLES

1

2

The commonest late Mycenaean idols known a Psi (1) and Phi (2) from their similarity to the Greek letters.

34

The cult centre at Mycenae

In recent years a cult centre with several shrines has been unearthed at Mycenae. One of these, the 'Room with Platforms', is shown on the left. This chapel was completely faced with white plaster. In the centre was a low dais, and at the far end several platforms of various heights. A goddess with an offerings table stood on one of these. On the right was a columned aisle with steps to a tiny room containing several broken statues and other things needed for the ceremonies.

Snake gods?

On the left side was a large window looking out onto the uncut rock face. This appears to have had some religious purpose as more broken statues were found outside the window. In all the remains of 23 idols and 17 mysterious clay snakes were found.

LEFT: a reconstruction of the 'Room with Platforms' at Mycenae. The roof and walls have been cut away to show the inside.
1 Statue and offerings table.
2 Stairs to store room.
3 Window. 4 Low dais.

BELOW: 5 An offerings table.
6 A grotesque female idol and a coiled snake. Both were found in the chapel.

BELOW: a burial scene from Hagia Triada. The corpse is propped up in front of the tomb while priests bring offerings. On the left a priestess prepares for the ceremony while a man plays the lyre.

Burial rites

In the Iliad the dead are cremated. This is true of the Trojans and also the Greeks of Homer's day, but it was not true of the Mycenaeans. They buried their dead in tombs. The most famous Mycenaean tomb is the so-called 'Treasury of Atreus' at Mycenae. This tomb (right) was built in the 13th century BC and was undoubtedly the tomb of a Mycenaean king, possibly even Agamemnon.

BELOW: a reconstruction of the Treasury of Atreus cut away to show the inside. The king's body was surrounded by his weapons, chariot horses and the food and drink needed for his journey to the underworld. The door was then closed and the passage filled in.

3

DAYS OF SORROW

Patroclus

Patroclus had been watching from afar. He was Achilles' squire and also his closest friend. As he watched the battle's progress his eyes filled with horror. Everywhere he looked he saw the mangled bodies of his friends. He begged Achilles to go to the rescue but still the great warrior refused. 'Then let me go,' implored Patroclus with tears streaming down his cheeks. 'Dressed in your armour and backed by your force of dreaded Myrmidons, at least I could take the pressure off our friends and give them a chance to recover.'

At last Achilles' heart softened. He took his own armour and dressed Patroclus in it, warning him, however, to fight only to save the ships and nothing more. Black smoke was billowing along the shore as Patroclus led Achilles' men into battle.

When the Trojans saw what appeared to be Achilles coming up on their flank followed by the blood-thirsty Myrmidons, their knees began to shake and they looked around for a way of escape. Achilles' name echoed down the lines as Patroclus charged into the Trojans striking them down with his spear. They fell back in disorder and with a great roar the Greeks dashed after them.

Patroclus, his work done, forgot Achilles' warning and raced after the fleeing Trojans. He pursued them across the river and all the way back to the walls of their city; it must have seemed to him that he could take Troy single handed, but when he tried to climb the walls Apollo hurled him down. He tried again and again but each time the god pushed him back. In disgust he turned and charged into the Trojan lines, killing whoever came his way.

But death was now stalking Patroclus. When he charged yet again Apollo struck him on the back. It was such a violent blow that it knocked his helmet off and shattered his spear in his hands. His shield fell from his shoulders and his armour tore apart. As he stood there in a daze, his body unprotected, a Trojan youth stabbed him in the back and brought him to his knees.

Hector, realizing at last that this was not Achilles, forced his way through the crowd to him. Wounded and defenceless Patroclus was trying desperately to crawl back to his own lines. Hector drove his spear into him shouting his victory cry.

'Don't boast of my death,' Patroclus told him with his dying breath, 'It took three of you; first a god, then a boy, and last of all you, Hector.'

The Trojan champion scornfully put his foot on Patroclus and pulled out his spear. He ordered his men to remove Achilles armour and, to the horror of his friends, prepared to dismember the body. He was interrupted by the arrival of Menelaus and Ajax. They drove Hector off but before they could carry Patroclus away Trojan reinforcements arrived and a bitter struggle developed over the corpse. The battle raged back and forth across the body as each side in turn gained possession of it. Gradually the Greeks managed to drag it towards their camp but the Trojans refused to give up the fight. Finally the Greeks sent a message to Achilles hoping that at last he would join the fight.

The Greek champion had sensed that something had gone wrong and he was filled with foreboding. When he was told that Patroclus was dead he flung himself on the ground consumed by despair. He poured dust in his hair, soiled his face and clothes and let out a hideous cry that was heard throughout the heavens. But he was powerless to do anything. He had no armour.

Thetis heard her son's cry of despair and hastened to Mount Olympus where she asked the divine smith, Hephaestus, to make a new set of armour as quickly as he could for Achilles.

Meanwhile the fight for Patroclus' body continued. Achilles was unable to join in but he went outside the rampart where he could watch the struggle. The Greeks had managed to drag the body most of the way to the camp but the Trojans were still determined to get it back. When Achilles saw Hector grab hold of Patroclus' foot and try to drag the body away again he yelled out his war-cry. Three times his great voice boomed out across the plain. The Trojans shuddered when they heard it and began to scuttle away like frightened dogs.

Hephaestus laboured all through the night and before dawn he had completed a magnificent set of armour for Achilles. The Greek champion had spent the night in tears but when Thetis arrived carrying the armour his thoughts turned to vengeance. He set off along the beach shouting to the Greeks calling them to the assembly. They all knew that the great moment had arrived and even Diomedes and Odysseus came limping in.

When all had assembled Achilles addressed Agamemnon: 'Forget our feud. Call the troops to battle.'

The soldiers shouted their approval. Agamemnon willingly apologised for what he had done. He promised to compensate Achilles and handed over the command of the whole army to him.

Odysseus was determined that Agamemnon should not go back on his word and insisted that the compensation be placed before the assembly. After this had been done Agamemnon sacrificed a boar to appease the gods, the soldiers breakfasted and they prepared for battle.

Patroclus forgot Achilles' orders and tried to capture Troy. Three times he tried to climb the walls but each time Apollo threw him down. In disgust Patroclus threw himself into the thick of the battle but death was awaiting him there.

Hector's last fight

Achilles' one desire was to kill Hector. When the Trojan champion did not come out to challenge him he turned his anger on the other Trojans and began to cut them down mercilessly. One of Hector's own brothers was an easy victim. Hector had been avoiding Achilles but when he saw his brother fall, he charged in angrily to avenge him.

Zeus had withdrawn his order preventing the gods taking sides and when Athena saw Hector's spear hurtling towards Achilles she blew it aside. Apollo thought this most unfair and when Achilles counter attacked he hid Hector in a dense mist and whisked him away. Achilles plunged his spear into the mist but struck nothing. Again and again he lunged into the mist and then swearing in frustration he turned on the other Trojans.

In his frenzy he crashed through the Trojan line scattering one half in the direction of the city while the rest fled for the ford. Many fell into the river in panic, and Achilles leapt after them slashing to the left and right until the river ran red with blood.

The carnage proved too much for the gods and with a great roar that shook the very heavens they joined in. Zeus chuckled with glee when he saw how they fought each other. Ares charged Athena and struck her on the chest with his spear but her tasselled cloak, the magic aegis, protected her. She picked up a massive rock and hurled it at 'the butcher' knocking him flat on his back. As she walked off laughing Aphrodite helped the war god to his feet but Athena ran after then and punched the love goddess on the chest with such force that she and Ares both collapsed in a heap on the ground.

King Priam had ordered the gates to be held open to receive the remnants of his routed forces. When they had all crowded in the gates were slammed and barred. Only Hector remained outside – waiting for Achilles.

Apollo had led the Greek champion off on a wild goose chase but now he came dashing back across the fields. Hector's mind was in a turmoil of doubt and fear. He knew that he could never face his people again if he did not stand up to Achilles. But he also knew that if he did he was doomed.

As Achilles approached the Scaean Gate where Hector was waiting, the Trojan's nerve broke. He turned and ran. Achilles was after him in a flash. He signalled to his men that this was a private fight and they were not to join in. The Greek hero used his greater speed to get between Hector and the walls,

cutting off all hope of escape. Nothing could save him now.

Even the gods watched in breathless silence as Achilles pursued Hector around the city. In his desperate flight the Trojan circled the city three times but he was unable to get away. Whenever he looked back over his shoulder Achilles was there like a hound close on the scent of a fox.

Finally he turned to face his pursuer. As Achilles closed in Hector tried to bargain with him: 'If Zeus gives victory to me I promise I will not mutilate your body. Will you make the same pledge?'

Achilles brushed aside his request scornfully: 'You must be mad, Hector. Friendship between us is impossible. Gather your courage together and fight for I intend to make you pay the full price for what you have done to me.'

Hector's parents and wife watched sickened with horror as Achilles dragged the body of the Trojan champion around the walls of the town.

With this Achilles hurled his heavy spear. Hector ducked, laughing as the weapon sailed harmlessly over his head and stuck in the ground behind him. 'You were too sure of yourself, Achilles. Dodge this one if you can'.

Hector flung his spear. It was a superb cast but Achilles caught it on his shield. Hector cursed, drew his sword and leapt towards Achilles. But even as he charged death stared him in the face. Athena had returned Achilles' spear. The point caught him in the neck and he crashed to the ground.

'Please,' Hector begged, as his life's blood soaked into the dust staining it dark purple, 'don't throw my body to the dogs.'

'Nothing will save you from the dogs, not even your weight in gold,' Achilles scowled at him.

Hector's strength was failing but he urged Achilles to think carefully before acting. 'You haven't long yourself. Don't risk offending the gods.'

Death punctuated Hector's words. Achilles pulled out his spear and began to strip the body whilst his men ran up and plunged their spears into the corpse. Achilles slit Hector's heels, passed a strap through the holes and attached it to his chariot. He then dragged the body round the town and off to the camp where he left it lying face down next to Patroclus' bier. Hector's mother, father and wife broke down as they watched this shameful scene from the battlements.

The following morning Patroclus' body was carried in state and placed on a huge pyre surrounded by sheep, cattle and horses. Jars of oil and honey and even two of Patroclus' dogs were added. But Achilles was still not satisfied and he threw twelve Trojan prisoners on too – an act of barbarity that shocked even his own side.

The pyre burned through the night. At dawn the flames were put out with wine and Patroclus' bones were recovered. They were sealed in a golden vase and buried beneath a mound of earth.

A double disaster

For eleven days Hector's body lay in the dust. Still Achilles' lust for vengeance remained unsatisfied. Occasionally he climbed into his chariot and dragged the body round Patroclus' tomb but he found no peace of mind.

On Mount Olympus the gods were becoming disturbed. In his life Hector had always shown due respect to the gods and he deserved better treatment than Achilles was meting out. Finally Apollo got Zeus to intervene. The great god, father of both gods and men, sent Thetis down to persuade her son to accept a ransom for the body.

Zeus also sent a message to king Priam telling him to load a cart with treasure, a fitting ransom for his son. That night the old king came down from Troy and the gods guided him silently through the Greek lines to Achilles' hut.

The old king, his hair and clothes dirty and dishevelled, burst into Achilles' hut unannounced and threw himself at Achilles' feet. He kissed the hands that had brought death to so many of his countrymen and begged pitifully for his son's body. 'Think of your own father,' he pleaded. 'He is much the same age as I am. Imagine how he would feel in my position. I have lost practically all my sons in this unending war.'

At first Achilles was too astonished to speak. His anger was still smouldering, but seeing the king humbled and broken, a spark of pity touched his heart. He helped the old man to his feet and ordered the maids to wash and clothe Hector's body before giving it to Priam. Then they unloaded the treasure and the king drove the corpse back to Troy where it was burned with full honours.

Patroclus was avenged and Hector was dead but the war was not over. Each dawn as the sun rose crimson from behind the eastern hills the two armies descended on to the plain to demand their daily toll of blood. And each evening as the sun sank into the sea they retired wearily to glory over their victories and mourn their dead.

Achilles remained the great champion of the Greeks. When old Nestor's son was killed he treated it as a personal loss and vowed to avenge the old man. He plunged into the battle with Odysseus and Ajax on either side. The Trojans panicked when they saw the three heroes and fled to the city with the Greeks hard on their heels. The Trojans fled through the Scaean Gate and before the doors could be closed the Greeks had crowded in with them.

At last after nine long years they were within the walls. Ahead of them was the steep paved street leading up to Priam's palace just as Odysseus remembered it. Behind them was the great wall with the tower rising high above it. They looked up to its lofty battlements and just caught a glimpse of Paris' laughing face with Apollo behind him. There was a dull thud and suddenly Achilles was writhing in the dust, a poisoned arrow sticking in his heel. Ajax and Odysseus covered him with their shields but within minutes he was dead.

In a state of shock Ajax heaved Achilles' body onto his broad shoulder and the two heroes beat a hasty retreat. As they withdrew through the gates the Trojans fell upon them like hungry wolves maddened by the smell of blood. Odysseus thrust out at them with his spear and held them at bay until they reached the safety of their own lines.

The Greeks were stunned. They gave their dead champion a magnificent funeral and placed his bones alongside those of his friend Patroclus. His sacred armour was awarded to Odysseus for the bravery he had shown in rescuing the body. It was a great honour but Odysseus' pleasure was short-lived.

Achilles' death was followed by another disaster. Ajax had been one of Odysseus' closest friends and had even saved his life once. Now his mind became twisted. He was insanely jealous because he had not received Achilles' armour. The great warrior could find no solace. Even his sleep was plagued by nightmares and finally he killed himself.

The death of the two heroes was a terrible loss to the Greeks but some weeks later they received some consolation as Paris, the true cause of all the war and sadness, met his death. Menelaus took great pleasure in mutilating his body. It seemed that at last it was all over but Aphrodite had one trick left to play. Paris' brother Deiphobus was also in love with Helen and he forced her to marry him.

Achilles fell to the ground with an arrow in his heel. According to legend this was the only place he could be wounded. Odysseus and Ajax covered him with their shields but within moments the great hero was dead.

The wooden horse

One morning the Trojans awoke to see a cloud of smoke hanging over the Greek camp. To their surprise they discovered that the Greeks had gone leaving their camp in ashes. The only thing that remained was a huge wooden statue of a horse dedicated to Athena.

The Trojans were mystified. What could it mean? Some wanted to drag the statue up to the citadel but others were highly suspicious and demanded that it be burnt. King Priam was loathe to desecrate the statue risking the wrath of the goddess. He ordered it to be hauled across the plain on rollers. When they reached the town they found that the statue was far too large to get through the gates and part of the walls had to be dismantled. The statue stuck four times but finally they got it through and rebuilt the wall behind them. Sweating in the heat of the day they laboriously began to haul the great statue up the steep street but they found the route blocked by Priam's strange but beautiful daughter Cassandra and the prophet Laocoön.

'It's full of men!' screamed Cassandra. But Priam's supporters shouted her down.

'She's mad! Everybody knows it!'

Priam ordered the men to continue.

'You fools! Never trust a Greek bringing gifts!' shouted Laocoön and hurled his spear at the horse. The weapon stuck quivering in the wood and there was a distinct clatter of metal inside the statue.

'Burn it,' screamed some of the mob. 'Hurl it over the walls.'

Amidst all the din and commotion a prisoner was being dragged up the street. It was Odysseus' cousin, Sinon. When the Greek saw Priam he threw himself at the old king's feet and begged his protection. He told the king how he had been hounded by Odysseus.

'Once we were close friends,' he sobbed, 'but since Ajax's death Odysseus has changed. He is now embittered and suspicious of all those around him. He accused me of being a coward and a cheat. He had me arrested and would have killed me if I hadn't escaped last night when they were launching the ships.'

Priam interrupted him.

'Tell us about the horse.'

Sinon explained that the Greeks had fallen foul of Athena.

'In fact that was the reason they gave up the siege. The horse was built to try to placate the angry goddess.'

'But why is it so big?' Priam asked.

'Oh,' Sinon laughed, 'that was so that you wouldn't be able to bring it into the city.'

Priam was convinced and ordered the horse to be dragged on up to the sanctuary of Athena where he dedicated it to the goddess. Girls went down into the plain to gather flowers along the river banks and made garlands to decorate the statue.

That evening Helen came to look at the horse. She walked round the huge statue occasionally tapping it and calling out the names of the various heroes. Then she turned and smiled at her husband, Deiphobus.

'Of course they aren't inside it,' she scoffed.

That night the Trojans held a great feast to celebrate their victory. Around midnight Odysseus' cousin, Sinon, slipped out and lit a beacon. The signal was seen on the heights of the island of Tenedos and passed on to Agamemnon who was waiting with the fleet. By the light of the moon the Greeks clambered aboard their ships and strained at their oars until the black hulls were skimming across the glittering water.

Unaware of the fate that awaited them the Trojans dragged the huge statue of a horse across the plain and up into the town.

The Trojans were still in a drunken slumber after their riotous night of celebrations. They did not see a door open in the belly of the horse nor did they see the shadowy figures climbing down with their armour glinting in the first light of dawn.

Some rushed to open the gates whilst others headed for the palace but Menelaus and Odysseus made straight for Helen's house. Menelaus killed Deiphobus the moment he saw him and viciously mutilated his body. He would have killed Helen too in his anger. But his heart melted when he saw her and he dropped his sword. He gathered her up in his arms and carried her through the gates and down to the ships. Odysseus set the house on fire and then joined the others. They had already broken into the palace and butchered the royal family, killing even Hector's infant son.

One of the Greeks broke into the temple of Athena and tried to carry off Cassandra. She threw her arms around the statue of Athena and cried out to the goddess for protection. The soldier tried to pull her away and the statue crashed to the ground, an act that would have far reaching consequences for the Greeks.

All the men, boys and old women were slaughtered and their houses set on fire. The young women and girls were dragged down to the ships where they would be shared out as booty. Only one man was spared; nine years earlier Antenor, then a member of the Trojan council, had saved Odysseus and Menelaus when they had gone to the city as ambassadors. Odysseus made sure that their debt to him was paid. Both his family and house were spared but everything else was handed over to the flames. It was all over in a few hours and the Greeks returned to their ships leaving the city blazing behind them.

Troy: The Plain

BELOW: a reconstruction of the plain of Troy seen from the south. The western (left) side of the plain is low lying and marshy. In the last 3,000 years the bay has silted up. The same thing has happened on a smaller scale at Besika Bay. The western side of the Sigean Promontary has been eroded by the sea (see map on right). At this time there would have been a plain about 1km wide to the west of Troy, where some of the fighting could have taken place.

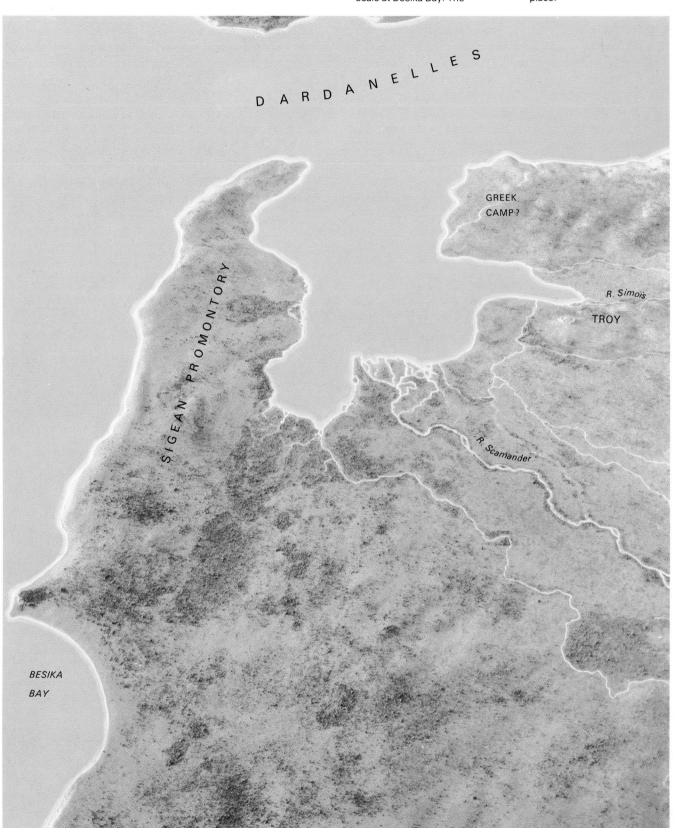

DARDANELLES

SIGEAN PROMONTORY

GREEK CAMP?

R. Simois

TROY

R. Scamander

BESIKA BAY

An illusion

A visitor standing on the hill of Troy can easily conjure up images of the Trojan war – the clash of shields, the shouts of triumph and the groans of death. Below the city a broad dusty plain stretches out towards the Dardanelles, the channel leading to the Black Sea. One can imagine the Greeks scrambling ashore and charging across the plain. But such images are false; 3,000 years have changed the plain beyond recognition.

A marshland

When Schliemann, the discoverer of Troy, first visited the site in 1868 it was far different. Rivers meandered across the plain and a great marsh on its western side made it unhealthy and difficult to cross. In winter the whole area was often flooded.

RIGHT: Map showing the gradual silting up of the Trojan Plain.

BELOW: view from the Rhoetean Ridge (the probable site of the Greek camp) looking across the valley of the Simoïs. Troy stood at the right end of the ridge in the middle distance. The dip in the distant hills is Besika Bay with the island of Tenedos just visible beyond it.

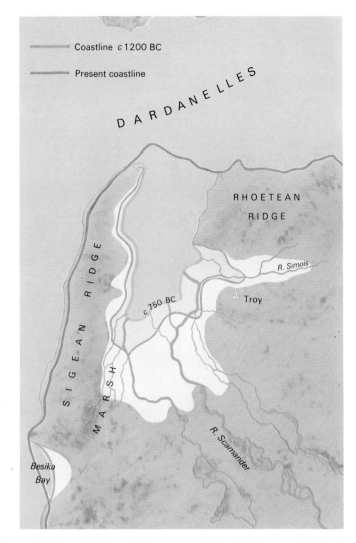

Coastline c 1200 BC

Present coastline

DARDANELLES

RHOETEAN RIDGE

S I G E A N   R I D G E

R. Simoïs

c 750 BC

Troy

M A R S H

R. Scamander

Besika Bay

The bay of Troy

This picture of a marshy plain liable to flooding is valid for 3,000 years ago too, but this is not the whole story. Recent tests show that the northern part of the plain was once a bay that has gradually silted up. The Sigean Ridge and the Rhoetean Ridge that hem in the plain today were once two promontaries. Troy itself was on a ridge jutting into the bay.

The changing plain

The map on the left shows the changes that have taken place over the last 4,500 years. The lightest blue area shows the extent of the plain when Troy was founded about 2,500 BC. The green line shows how much the bay had shrunk by 1,200 BC. The light blue line shows its probable size in Homer's time. The red line shows the modern coast.

The rivers

The Trojan plain is scored with river beds caused by the constantly changing course of the river Scamander. Homer says the Simoïs, which must be the stream to the north of Troy, joined the Scamander. This was possible in Homer's day but not during the Trojan war.

A naval power?

Troy's powerful position close to the Dardanelles, with a natural haven for ships, suggests that the city was a naval power. The fabled wealth of Troy was probably collected as toll money from ships using the Dardanelles. This is the most likely cause of the war with the Greeks, as they were trying to trade along the coast of the Black Sea.

The Greek camp

There are two possible sites for the Greek camp – Besika Bay and the south-western corner of the Rhoetean Promontary. Both are protected from the prevailing north-east wind and both have space for beaching ships. Besika Bay is opposite the island of Tenedos from which the Greeks launched both their first and last attacks on Troy. But it is nearly 9km from Troy and the approach is accross the marshes of the Scamander. The Rhoetean Promontary is only about 3km from Troy and seems far more likely.

Troy: The Excavations

RIGHT: reconstruction of Troy at the end of the sixth period from the east side. The flooded plain is in the background.

BELOW: the north east bastion.

BELOW RIGHT: The tower, east wall and gate of Troy VI.

The excavators

Troy was discovered by an amateur archaeologist, Heinrich Schliemann, in 1870. He found several towns each built on the ruins of the previous one. At the second level up he discovered signs of burning and concluded that this was Homer's Troy.

In 1882 Schliemann was joined by a professional archaeologist, Wilhelm Dörpfeld, and the excavating was soon left to him. Dörpfeld identified nine successive towns on the site and was able to show that Homer's Troy was between the sixth and seventh levels.

Dörpfeld's findings were checked by an American expedition between 1932 and 1938. They agreed with his findings but improved techniques enabled them to identify no less than 30 different levels of occupation.

Homer's Troy

How did Schliemann manage to miss Homer's Troy and dig down to a town built 1,000 years earlier (for towns were built one on top of the other)? The constant rebuilding had formed a mound. The top of this mound was levelled when the 9th town was built to construct a sanctuary to Athena. In doing this the centre of several of the preceding towns was destroyed. Schliemann, digging down in the centre of the mound, could never have guessed that there was a 6th 7th and 8th town. Dörpfeld extended his trenches outwards and discovered traces of terracing to level up the slope (see below, number 4), and the monumental walls of the 6th town further down the hillside.

The great walls of Troy

Most of the eastern wall still stands to a height of about 4m. It is some 4.5m thick. The wall slopes back considerably and could be climbed quite easily, but it was topped by an upright superstructure which rose another 3–4m.

The eastern wall was reinforced by a tower. A massive bastion at the north-east corner was built to defend a well which was the main water supply.

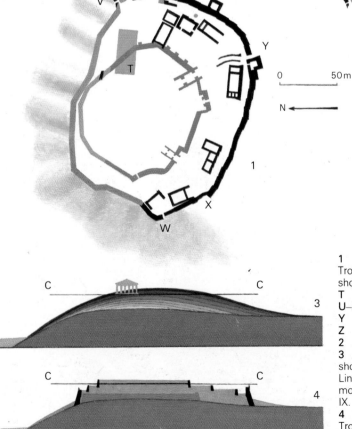

1   Plan of Troy VIh (black) and Troy II (red). The wells are shown in blue.
T   The later temple of Athena.
U–Z   The gates.
Y   The Scaean Gate?
Z   the Dardanian Gate?
2   Plan of Troy VIIa.
3   Section of the mound showing the eight first levels. Line C–C shows where the mound was levelled off for Troy IX.
4   Reconstructed section of Troy VIh showing its terraces. Troy II is shown in red.

Troy: The Siege

Which Troy?

Experts disagree over which Troy was destroyed by the Mycenaeans. Was it VIh, a powerful and wealthy town with spacious well constructed buildings? This fits Homer's description but it appears to have been destroyed by an earthquake. Or was it VIIa, the new town that rose out of the rubble.

Troy VIIa

Troy VIIa was poor and over-populated. It was destroyed by fire after a life of only about 30 years. Its crudely built houses were huddled against the town walls. Most had large pots (pithoi) buried in the floor for storing food.
These features indicate a siege mentality, with the people from the countryside crowding into the town for protection.

ABOVE: a model of a Hittite tower in the Istanbul museum.

RIGHT: a reconstruction of the south tower and gate of Troy VI and VII. This was probably the Scaean Gate.

BELOW: a model of Troy and its immediate surroundings seen from the east. It was built on the end of a spur with a steep incline along its north side.

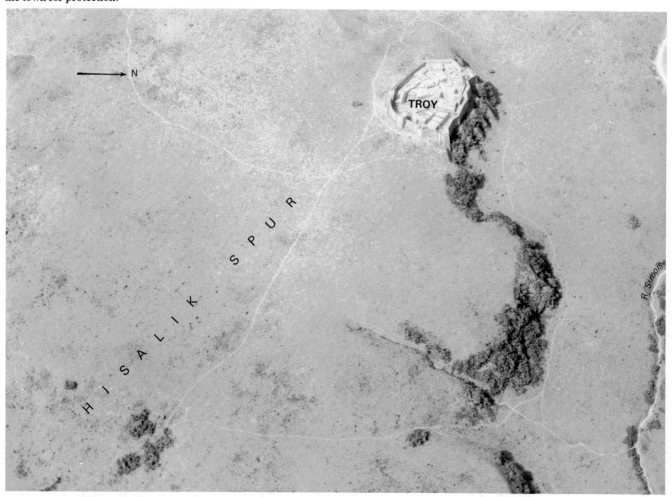

RIGHT AND LEFT: plans of the gates of Troy VI to VII.

1 The south gate (Y) and tower. This is probably the Scaean gate where Achilles was killed.

2 South-west gate (W).

3 South-west gate (X) blocked late in the sixth period.

4 Sally ports (V and U) leading from the north-east bastion. The well is shown in blue.

5 The eastern gate (Z) during the VIh period.

6 The defences of the eastern gate improved during the VIIa period.

BELOW: a reconstruction of the fortifications of Troy VIIa between the east tower and the east gate. The walls and ground have been cut away to show the construction. The tower was built on solid rock but the wall was cushioned on a layer of earth. The lower wall was backed by the debris of the previous towns, making it impervious to battering rams. The houses backed onto the wall. Two pithoi (P,P) are buried in the floor. Others covered by stone slabs are behind.

The defences of Troy VIIa

The buildings within Troy VIIa were far poorer than those of its predecessor, but the defences of the town were actually stronger. The sloping base of the old wall appears to have remained intact after the earthquake but the superstructure had to be rebuilt.

The eastern gate

Along the eastern wall which is the only part that can really be studied, several changes were made. The eastern gate was reinforced with two towers or bastions. A wall was built to force any attackers to advance under a murderous barrage of missiles, first from the main eastern tower, then from the town wall, and finally from the towers or bastions flanking the gates.

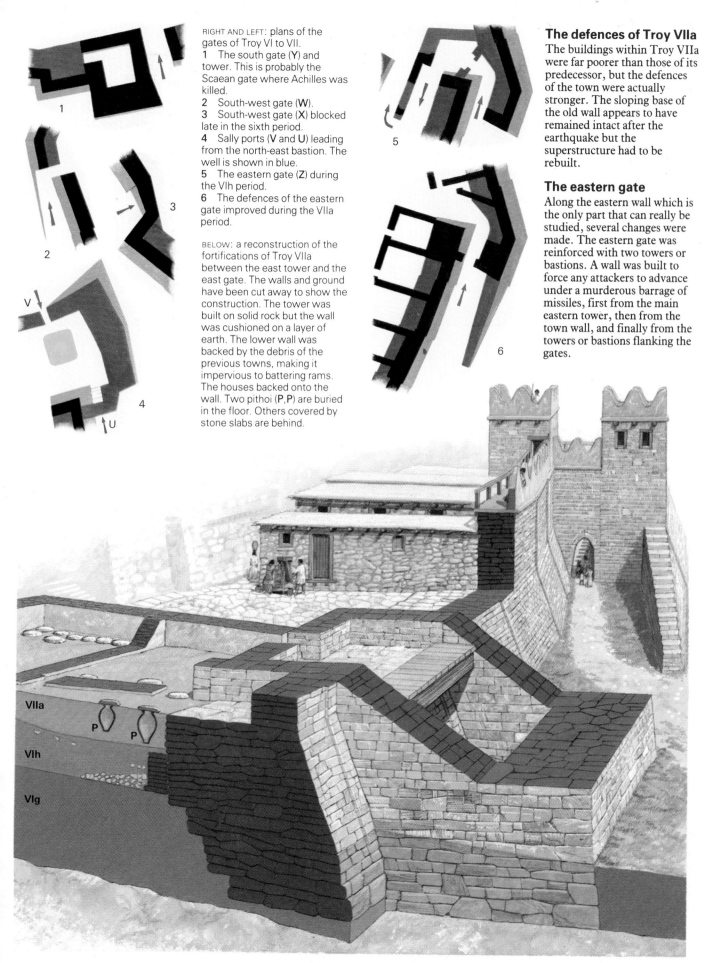

THE GREAT ADVENTURE

The return of the Heroes

The war was over and the Greeks prepared to sail home. But Athena had not forgotten the violation of her temple.

Agamemnon and Menelaus could not agree what should be done. Agamemnon insisted that they stay where they were and offer sacrifices to try to placate the angry goddess. Menelaus believed that their first duty was to get their troops back to Greece. When the sun set and no agreement had been reached they called an assembly and put the matter to the troops. The soldiers had been celebrating their victory and drinking heavily. Tempers were short and the assembly ended in uproar. Half the army put to sea while the rest remained behind. Odysseus, Menelaus, Diomedes and Nestor, all old friends, set out for home. But when they reached Tenedos Odysseus made a fateful decision. He concluded Agamemnon was right and turned back. Nestor and Diomedes sailed on and reached home in a few days. They were the lucky ones.

Menelaus had reached the southernmost point of Greece, the treacherous Cape Malea, when he was hit by a storm. His fleet was driven south-east towards Crete where he lost most of his ships. Finally, with only five vessels left, he reached Egypt where he was marooned.

Agamemnon, Odysseus and the rest of the army offered sacrifices to Athena and then set out for home. But the goddess could not be appeased so easily and many of the Greeks found a watery grave.

Agamemnon sailed back to Greece never dreaming of the fate that awaited him there. He had no idea that his wife had been unfaithful. When he reached home he was met by her lover Aegisthus who had prepared a banquet to celebrate the king's return. After the feast twenty of Aegisthus' men ambushed the king and his companions. Agamemnon fought them off savagely and the floor of the great hall ran with blood. But finally the king and all his companions were overwhelmed.

Agamemnon had a young son, Orestes, who mysteriously disappeared after the massacre. Aegisthus searched desperately for the boy as he had to kill him if he was to avoid a vendetta when the boy grew up. But he was nowhere to be found.

Odysseus set out from Troy at the same time as Agamemnon. He sailed north-west to the Thracian coast where he sighted the town of Ismarus which had been an ally of the Trojans. He sacked the town and celebrated his victory with a feast by the shore. At dawn they were attacked by the Thracians and only managed to escape with the loss of seventy-two men. As they sailed away they were caught in a dreadful storm and driven southwards for two days and nights. On the third day the storm vanished and they were able to head for home once again. But as they were rounding the treacherous headland of Malea, where Menelaus had been driven off course, another storm hit them. They were blown southwards past the island of Cythera and out into the unknown sea and far beyond.

A dreadful storm hit Odysseus'
ships as they were rounding the
treacherous Cape of Malea, and
drove them out into the
unknown sea.

Penelope

All through those long years of war Penelope had waited faithfully for Odysseus. One by one the other heroes returned but there was never a word of Odysseus. As months dissolved into years all hope faded. She knew in her heart that he was dead and night after night she cried herself to sleep.

Soon the young nobles began to court the bereaved queen. At first Penelope was flattered but she politely rejected their advances. However they would not accept the rebuff and became more and more aggressive until their courtship developed into a siege.

Penelope tried desperately to put them off but rejection only made them more arrogant and persistent. She knew that she could not hold out for ever so she devised a scheme that was worthy of Odysseus himself. She told the suitors that she would accept one of them but they would have to wait until she had woven a shroud for Odysseus' father who could not be expected to live many more years. The suitors could hardly refuse and Penelope began to weave the great sheet. At first it grew quite rapidly, and then not so rapidly, until at last no one was quite sure whether it was getting bigger or smaller.

For three years Penelope managed to keep the suitors waiting for the last stitch. Finally she was betrayed by one of her maids who told the suitors that she was unpicking the shroud at night. The suitors were furious and demanded that she make an immediate decision. When she refused they took over the palace. Every day they gathered in the great hall and entertained themselves at her expense. They ate her food, drank her wine and secretly plotted the murder of the only person who could foil their plans – her son Telemachus.

Telemachus was now nineteen. He was outraged at the treatment of both his mother and their property but he felt unable to do anything. It seemed that the house of Odysseus was doomed to extinction. But they still had one ally. Athena had not forgotten Odysseus or his family. She appeared to Telemachus and told him to go to Pylos and Sparta to see if there was any news of his father. The prince slipped out of the palace under cover of darkness and set sail for Pylos.

Nestor received Telemachus warmly but there was little that the old king could tell him. He lent him a chariot with one of his sons as driver and sent him on to Sparta.

For nineteen long years Penelope had waited for Odysseus to return, but no word had been heard of him since he had set out from Troy.

They talked late into the night but even so Menelaus rose at dawn and went to see his young guest. Telemachus poured out his unhappy story and the king flushed with anger when he heard of the state of things in Ithaca. 'Oh, shame on them,' he shouted. 'So the cowards are trying to steal that brave man's wife. When the lion returns to his lair he'll deal with them. There will be such bloodshed as you have never seen.'

'Then he is alive!' exclaimed Telemachus sitting up excitedly.

'I think so,' Menelaus replied. 'Only a few months ago I heard that he was being held prisoner on some distant island. Yes, knowing Odysseus as I do, I'm sure of it. He'll be back.'

A one-eyed giant

Even as Menelaus and Telemachus were talking the body of a shipwrecked sailor was being washed up on an island not so very far away. The exhausted wretch dragged himself clear of the water and collapsed under some bushes. He was a broad-shouldered man with auburn hair. He had two jagged scars – one on his hip and one above the knee. In spite of his haggard appearance and the salt that discoloured his hair and skin, it was not difficult to recognise the long lost king of Ithaca.

Some hours later he was found by a young princess who brought him to the palace where he was graciously received by her mother and father. The king agreed to provide Odysseus with a ship to take him home but begged him first to tell them of his adventures. This was the story he told.

"Nine years ago I was making my way home from Troy when my ships were caught in a gale. For many days we were blown helplessly across the unknown sea until one night we ran aground on an island. As the mainland was not far away I decided to take my ship with twelve men and explore.

"We discovered a cave full of sheep and goats carefully penned in. My men wanted to carry off the animals but I was curious and determined to see what sort of people lived there. So we waited in the cave until at last we heard someone approaching. An enormous figure filled the entrance. We cowered in the shadows at the back of the cave hoping he wouldn't notice us. The giant closed the entrance behind him with a huge rock and tended to his animals in the darkness. When he had finished he lit a fire and for the first time we saw his face.

"He was a Cyclops. The grotesque monster glared at us with his one eye and demanded to know who we were.

'We are soldiers returning from the war,' I explained. 'Please receive us according to the laws of hospitality laid down by the gods.'

'We don't care about the gods,' the Cyclops laughed.

"Then he seized two of my men, dashed their heads against the floor, tore off their arms and legs and ate them. We screamed in horror but there was nothing we could do.

"The Cyclops washed down his ghastly meal with milk and stretched out to sleep. I was tempted to draw my sword and try to kill him but I realized that even if I succeeded we would be trapped in the cave as we couldn't move the stone blocking the entrance. So we were forced to spend the night huddled together at the back of the cave quivering in terror.

"The Cyclops rose at dawn, rekindled the fire and saw to his animals. He then seized two more of my men. After he had eaten them he let the sheep and the goats out of the cave and closed it from the outside.

My men drove the smouldering stake into the Cyclops' eye, while I twisted it from above.

"I racked my brain for a plan of escape. There was just one faint glimmer of hope. Lying on the floor was a huge pole. I cut off a piece about two metres long, sharpened it to a point and put it in the fire to harden.

"When the Cyclops returned at sun-set he seized two more of my men for his supper. I offered him some wine which we had brought up from the ship. It was very strong and supposed to be diluted with twenty times the amount of water. But the Cyclops seized the bowl and drained it.

'What's your name?' he asked. I ignored his question for the moment and refilled the bowl.

"After the third dose his head began to swim.
'My name is Nobody,' I told him.

"He grunted and fell back in a drunken sleep. We immediately got out the stake and put its point in the fire. When it was red hot four of my men drove it into the Cyclops' eye while I twisted round from above.

"The Cyclops let out a piercing scream that echoed round the cave. We jumped back in terror as he tore the blazing stake from his eye and screamed to the other Cyclopses who lived in the neighbouring caves. They crowded outside clamouring to know what the trouble was.

'Nobody is attacking me,' he shrieked.

"The other Cyclopses concluded that he must be mad and went home again.

"The Cyclops fumbled his way around the cave until he found the way out. He pushed the rock aside and sat down in the entrance determined to catch us if we tried to escape. I made a plan. At the back of the cave he had some thick fleeced black rams. I tied them together in threes side by side and secured my men up underneath the one in the centre.

"At dawn the rams scrambled out of the cave while the ewes bleated to be milked. The Cyclops felt all the animals carefully as they passed him but never noticed my men tied up underneath. The last ram to reach the Cyclops was the largest and I was hanging on upside down beneath it. It was the Cyclops favourite and he fondled it and spoke to it tenderly.

'Why are you so late, my love. You are usually first.'

"I thought I was discovered and my whole body was gripped with fear but the Cyclops thought no more about it and let the animal by.

"As soon as I was outside I released my companions. We quickly drove the animals down to the ship and hauled them aboard. As we pulled away from the shore I shouted back to the Cyclops taunting him:

'I was not such a weakling as you thought – was I?'

"The angry giant seized a massive rock and hurled it at us. It overshot and hit the water ahead of us but its backwash almost drove us ashore again. I managed to push the ship clear and my men rowed for all they were worth. When we were well out from the shore I couldn't resist another jibe at the Cyclops. My men tried to stop me but I was determined to have my say.

'Cyclops,' I shouted back, 'If anyone wants to know how you lost your eye, tell them it was Odysseus the king of Ithaca who did it.'

"The Cyclops let out a dreadful groan and raised his hands towards the heavens.

'Poseidon, my father,' he prayed, 'avenge me for the evil this man has done to me.'

'Then he picked up another rock and hurled it in our direction. The rock hit the water behind us and drove the ship further from the shore. We escaped but the Cyclops was to have his revenge.'

The valley of death

"We sailed on for many days and finally reached the land of the Laestrygonians where the nights are very short. My captains dropped anchor in a natural harbour surrounded by steep cliffs but I stayed just outside the entrance and moored my ship to a rock. I climbed up the cliff to see if I could get my bearings. In the distance I could just see a wisp of smoke so I sent three men to find out whether the land was inhabited or not.

"The three men soon found a cart track which led them to a village where they found a rather large girl drawing water from the well. She directed them to the chief's house and suspecting nothing they went in. They were met by a colossal woman whose very appearance filled them with dread. Before they could escape she had called her husband. He pounced on them and managed to grab one but the other two got away.

"They raced back to the ships but before my captains could draw up their anchors, thousands of huge men appeared on top of the cliffs and started bombarding my ships with boulders. I could hear the screams of my men above the splintering of the timbers. It was appalling. And then, one by one these monsters harpooned my men like fish and carried them home to eat.

"Fortunately I was moored outside the harbour. I slashed the hawser and yelled to my crew to row for their lives. We got away but all the others perished.

"We sailed on and on in despair never finding our way home. Finally we reached the very frontiers of the world, a land of perpetual mist where the light of day is never seen. We had been directed here by a witch who insisted that only the blind prophet Teiresias could show us the way home – and he was dead. So we had come to the underworld in search of him.

"We beached our ship and trudged through the eery half light until we reached the spot where the River of Flaming Fire and the River of Sadness thunder down on either side of a great rock to form the River of Woe.

"Here I dug a pit, poured wine around it and sprinkled the area with barley. I sacrificed two sheep and let their blood drain into the pit. We heard a dreadful moaning and the souls of the dead began to rise. I was terrified. I shouted to my men to skin and burn the sacrificial animals as quickly as possible. Meanwhile I sat by the pit, sword in hand, making sure that none of the other spirits drank the blood before I had spoken to the blind prophet. I saw my mother. I didn't even knew she was dead and I longed to take her in my arms but I had to drive her away.

"At last the prophet appeared. I sheathed my sword and invited him to drink the blood. He directed me home but warned me that my journey would not be easy.

'Poseidon is determined to avenge the Cyclops so watch for him. And do not touch the Sun-god's cattle when you pass the island of Thrinacie. Give it a wide berth. Do as I say and you may reach Ithaca. But if you do, you will find trouble there too.'

"When the prophet had gone I called my mother. I tried to take her in my arms but she slipped through them like a shadow. I cried out to her in despair; 'Mother, why do you avoid me?'

'My child,' she replied, 'don't worry about me. Remember all that you have learned here so that one day you will be able to reach home and tell Penelope.'

"A great horde of shadowy figures had collected ⌐ the blood and I spoke to many of them. ⌐⌐⌐⌐ ⌐⌐as there and Achilles too with Patroclus. I s⌐⌐⌐ ⌐ut he refused to talk to me. The spirits crowded arou⌐ d me with their hideous cries. My skin crawled. I lost my nerve and ran."

Amidst dreadful moaning the spirits of the dead began to rise. I saw my mother coming towards me — I didn't even know she was dead. With tears in my eyes I drove her back. I had to see Teiresias.

57

A whirlpool and a monster

"When we reached the ship I told my men what lay ahead and warned them in particular of the Sirens whom we would encounter first. They have the most beautiful voices and lure sailors ashore with their songs. Their island is littered with the dead bodies of these unfortunate men. I had been told how I could hear their songs and still survive.

"As we approached the island the wind dropped. the crew lowered the sail and ran out the oars. While they rowed I went round plugging their ears with wax. Then they bound me to the mast and returned to their oars. Soon I heard sweet voices calling to me across the water. They called my name. Their alluring sound was more than I could bear. I signalled to my men to release me but they only bound me tighter and strained at the oars until those seductive voices faded in the distance.

"My men had barely released me when we saw a cloud of black smoke. We were approaching the mountain of the dreaded Scylla whose peak is always shrouded in dark smoke. The Scylla is a twelve footed monster with six long necks each ending in a fearsome head with three rows of teeth. It lives in a cave half way up the mountain. I had been told that there was no defence against the Scylla as no arrow could reach its cave. Nevertheless, I armed myself and stood at the front of the ship. I ordered the helmsman to hug the mountain. I knew this was leaving us wide open to the Scylla but anything was better than being dragged down by the Charybdis.

"The Charybdis lies opposite the Scylla. It is a whirlpool which sucks down the dark waters and then throws them up again. It is situated at the foot of a cliff crowned by a huge fig tree.

"We sailed up the strait, hugging the sheer face of the mountain and gazing in horror at the whirlpool as it sucked down the water and spurted it up again drenching the cliffs with spray. As we rowed desperately along its perimeter we could see right down into its vortex to the bed of the sea itself. My gaze was transfixed in terror. Suddenly I heard someone screaming my name and I looked up to see six of my men dangling in the air above me. For a moment I heard their screams and then there was silence. The Scylla had taken its toll.

"The horror was over. We were now approaching the island of Thrinacie. The blind prophet had warned me to avoid it but my men were verging on mutiny after their last experience so I agreed to let them camp overnight on the beach as long as each man swore an oath not to touch the Sun-god's cattle.

"That night a storm broke and I knew that we were likely to be stuck on the island several days. We had plenty of food with us and we would not go hungry. But the gales lasted for a month. Our food ran out and finally the pangs of hunger overcame my men's scruples. They ate some of the Sun-god's cattle.

"When the winds dropped we put to sea. Clouds gathered and we were hit by a violent storm. The rigging was ripped apart and the mast fell on the helmsman. Lightning struck the ship and finally a great wave ripped the sides apart. We were plunged into the water and that was the last I saw of my companions.

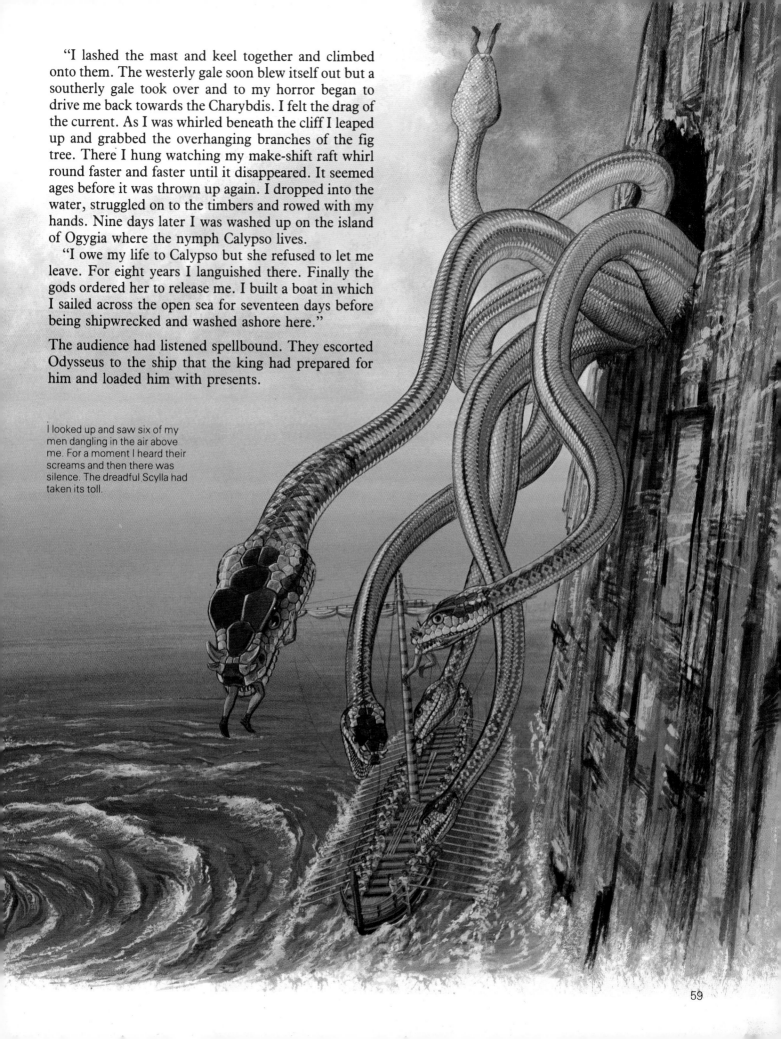

"I lashed the mast and keel together and climbed onto them. The westerly gale soon blew itself out but a southerly gale took over and to my horror began to drive me back towards the Charybdis. I felt the drag of the current. As I was whirled beneath the cliff I leaped up and grabbed the overhanging branches of the fig tree. There I hung watching my make-shift raft whirl round faster and faster until it disappeared. It seemed ages before it was thrown up again. I dropped into the water, struggled on to the timbers and rowed with my hands. Nine days later I was washed up on the island of Ogygia where the nymph Calypso lives.

"I owe my life to Calypso but she refused to let me leave. For eight years I languished there. Finally the gods ordered her to release me. I built a boat in which I sailed across the open sea for seventeen days before being shipwrecked and washed ashore here."

The audience had listened spellbound. They escorted Odysseus to the ship that the king had prepared for him and loaded him with presents.

I looked up and saw six of my men dangling in the air above me. For a moment I heard their screams and then there was silence. The dreadful Scylla had taken its toll.

The Voyages of Odysseus

The Greek view

The Iliad and the Odyssey were sacred books to most Greeks. Yet the wanderings of Odysseus were a subject of heated argument even in those days.

The earlier Greeks believed that the places mentioned were to be found in the western Mediterranean. This area was little known even though Mycenaean ships had traded along the coasts of Italy and Sicily.

Beyond Gibraltar

Later, as Greek traders opened up the western Mediterranean, establishing colonies on the coast of Spain, people began to look beyond the Straits of Gibraltar for Odysseus' wonderland. But many now concluded that the search was hopeless and dismissed the whole story as pure fiction.

RIGHT: the central area of the Mediterranean showing some of the places thought to be connected with the voyages of Odysseus.

BELOW: map of the eastern Mediterranean and the Black Sea. In late Mycenaean times Greek trading ships had been opening up the Black Sea. It seems very reasonable to place the entrance to the underworld on the coast of the Sea of Azov, the northern-most point of the Black Sea. It must have seemed like the end of the world to the Greeks and fits Homer's description well.

Ismarus

DARDANELLES
Troy

AEGEAN SEA

CORFU

ACHERON G R E E C E

LEVKAS

ITHACA

CEPHALONIA

Pylos • • Sparta

CAPE MALEA

CRETE

Y A N S E A

The modern view

Time has not altered things much. The same three groups still exist today. There are those who still believe that it was a local affair limited to the Mediterranean.

The second group, with its greater knowledge of geography, has been able to take Odysseus even further afield. He has now sailed into the north Atlantic and circumnavigated Africa. These claims may not be quite as absurd as they seem. Both the Egyptians and the Carthaginians sailed round Africa long before the birth of Jesus, and recently there have been reports of a Roman shipwreck off the coast of South America.

Pure fiction?

The author is one of the third group believing Odysseus' adventures to be pure fiction. But Homer does appear to be using 'travellers tales' for his details, though he makes no attempt to locate them. Therefore it seems pointless to assume that the island of the Sirens for example had to be near the Scylla and Charybdis. For the sake of argument let us follow the clues and see where they lead.

Lost at Sea

We lose track of Odysseus and his ships when they round the treacherous Cape Malea at the southern tip of Greece. Here they were caught by a gale and driven out into the Libyan Sea. Ancient seamen having no compasses preferred to hug the coast and not to sail out of sight of land. In the Aegean Sea with its myriad of tiny islands it is almost impossible to be out of sight of land. But the Libyan Sea is quite different. bounded by Sicily, Crete and the north coast of Africa, it is the largest stretch of open water in the eastern Mediterranean. The early sailors were justifiably frightened of it.

The Laestrygonians

It is impossible to locate the land of the Cyclopses as absolutely no check points are given. The land of the Laestrygonians is a far different matter. Homer says: 'In this land dusk and dawn tread so closely on each other's heels that a man who could do without sleep might earn a double set of wages'. The poet has to be describing the short summer nights of the far north, and many scholars have suggested Scandinavia.

The land of the Cimmerians

Homer says the Odysseus called up the spirits of the dead in the land of the Cimmerians. In the 7th century BC the Cimmerians lived north of the Black Sea. To an early Greek this would certainly be the end of the world and in many ways it fits Homer's description, but Odysseus would have had to sail back past Troy and through the Dardanelles to get there.·

In northern waters

For those who place the Laestrygonians in Scandinavia, the land of the Cimmerians has to be somewhere in these northern waters too. Ireland and even Iceland have been suggested. Ireland could well be described as the land of perpetual mist, and Iceland has rivers of flaming fire pouring from its volcanoes.

Closer to home

Many Greeks believed that Lake Averno, in the volcanic area just north of Naples, was the entrance to the underworld. Recently Acheron on the west coast of Greece has been suggested. An oracle of the dead has been found here, but it is only 100km from Ithaca.

The Scylla and the Charybdis

Since the earliest times the Scylla and Charybdis have been placed on either side of the narrow strait of Messina between Sicily and the toe of Italy. Here the currents are treacherous.

The Scylla may be a slight misplacing of Mount Etna, 75km farther down the coast. It regularly erupts sending out lava flows and usually has a cloud of smoke hanging over its summit. A group of lava flows could have given rise to the Scylla story.

Vulcano in the Lipari Islands has also been suggested. It fits the description well, but Odysseus could have avoided the area by sailing round it.

Scherie

Odysseus was ship-wrecked on Scherie on the final leg of his journey home. It was here that he told the story of his adventures. It was only a few hours sailing from Ithaca and must surely be Corfu.

However, some people claim that ancient and modern Ithaca are not the same place (see page 76). It has been claimed that Homer's Ithaca is the west end of Sicily.

Old Nestor's Palace at Pylos

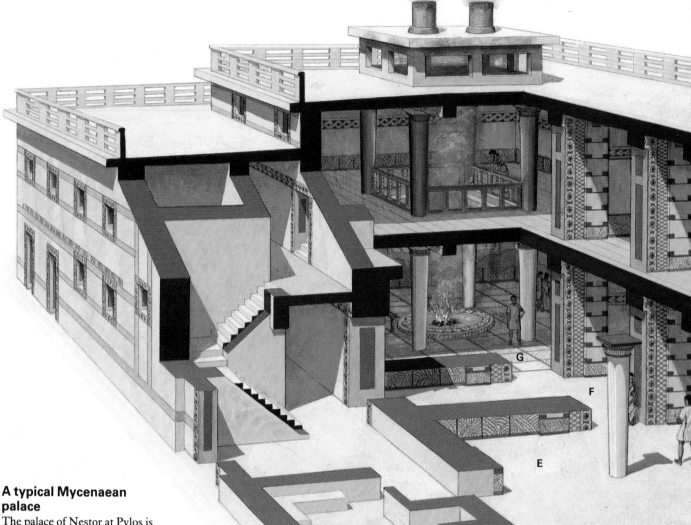

A typical Mycenaean palace

The palace of Nestor at Pylos is the most complete Mycenaean palace yet discovered. It was built on a flat topped hill, a few miles north-east of the bay of Pylos.

The palace was entered through a gateway with a double porch (A,B). To the right of the entrance was a small room (C), probably a guardroom. The gateway led into an open courtyard (D). Opposite was a columned porch (E) leading to a vestibule (F) and then on into the columned throne room or megaron (G). Along the sides of the megaron were corridors leading to the pantries, wine stores, kitchens and other service rooms. The megaron at Pylos has a typical design, with a circular hearth in the centre surrounded by four columns which supported the upper floor. The smoke from the fire passed through a hole in the ceiling and out through chimneys in the roof.

The queen's quarters

On the right side of the courtyard was another columned porch (H). To the left it led to the service rooms but on the right to a group of rooms that probably formed the queen's quarters. These included an uncolumned megaron (J), a boudoir and a toilet.

Next to the queen's megaron was a bathroom (K). This must have been for general use as there is no direct access to it from the queen's quarters.

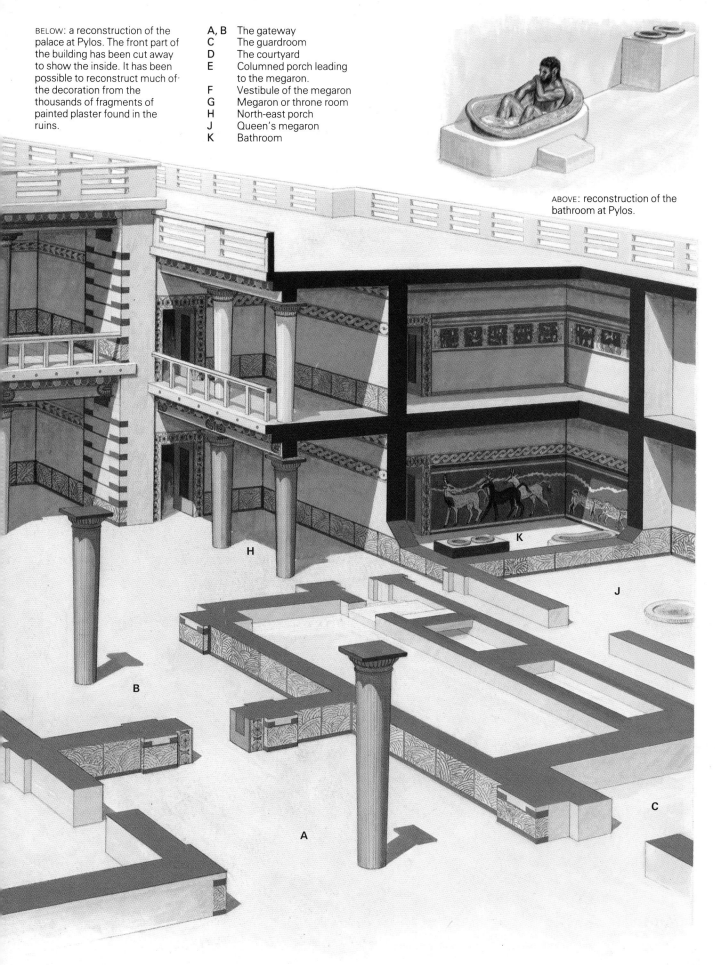

BELOW: a reconstruction of the palace at Pylos. The front part of the building has been cut away to show the inside. It has been possible to reconstruct much of the decoration from the thousands of fragments of painted plaster found in the ruins.

A, B   The gateway
C   The guardroom
D   The courtyard
E   Columned porch leading to the megaron.
F   Vestibule of the megaron
G   Megaron or throne room
H   North-east porch
J   Queen's megaron
K   Bathroom

ABOVE: reconstruction of the bathroom at Pylos.

5

THE HOMECOMING

Telemachus returns

Meanwhile, in Sparta, Telemachus had spent a restless night pondering the fate of his father. Was it possible that he was still alive? Athena appeared to him in his dreams and urged him to return home quickly but she warned him that the suitors had laid an ambush for him in the channel between Ithaca and Cephalonia.

At dawn he bid a hasty farewell to Menelaus and Helen and set out for Pylos. He went straight to his ship and ordered it to be dragged down to the sea. Just as he was setting sail he was approached by a stranger who claimed that he had killed a man and was fleeing the vengeance of the victim's family. It was a common occurrence. Telemachus offered the stranger shelter and invited him aboard.

Telemachus headed for Raven's Crag at the south-eastern end of Ithaca to avoid the ambush that the suitors had laid for him. His father's faithful old herdsman lived there.

The young prince heeded Athena's warning and ordered his men to head directly up the coast avoiding the Ithaca channel. They sailed right through the night and by dawn they were off the south east point of Ithaca heading for a place known as Raven's Crag where Odysseus' faithful old herdsman Eumaeus lived. The prince climbed up to Eumaeus' cottage and found the swineherd breakfasting with an old beggar.

Eumaeus welcomed him as if he were his own son. Telemachus nodded inquiringly towards the old beggar: 'Who is he?'

'He's only a beggar down on his luck,' Eumaeus explained. 'He spent the night here. He's a great story teller. He says he fought in the Trojan war but since then he's become a homeless wanderer.'

Eumaeus did not tell Telemachus that the stranger claimed to know Odysseus and insisted that the king was on his way home. He did not want to raise Telemachus' hopes. He liked the old traveller, but he certainly could not believe all his stories. Every beggar coming to the island claimed to have news of Odysseus; it was a guarantee of a free meal and fresh clothes at the palace.

The prince stayed at the cottage overnight and the following morning set out for the palace telling Eumaeus to bring the old man to town where he could beg more easily.

The prince collected the stranger from Pylos – he had sailed on to the town after they had parted the previous morning – and went up to the palace. After they had bathed and eaten, Telemachus told his mother what Menelaus had said. The queen hardly disguised her disbelief but the stranger insisted that it was true:

'Believe me,' he assured her, 'if only you could read the signs you would knew that Odysseus is not only alive but he is actually here on Ithaca.'

For nine years Penelope had waited for such news. In those years there had been many cruel reports of Odysseus' return. Why should this one be different? She thanked the stranger but remained unconvinced.

Just outside the town they fell foul of the bully Melanthius. He hurled abuse at them and kicked the old beggar as he passed.

That afternoon Eumaeus and the old beggar also arrived. As they passed the public fountain just outside the town they met another herdsman, Melantheus. In the king's absence he had become an insolent bully. When he saw them coming up the track he shouted abuse at them and kicked the beggar as he passed. The old man cursed under his breath but did not retaliate.

Odysseus' old hunting dog Argus lay in the yard outside the palace. He had been scarcely more than a puppy when the king had left nineteen years ago. Those years had taken their toll. When he had become too old for hunting he had been thrown out and left to die. He now lay half asleep amongst the piles of mule dung. He was in an appalling state and his fur was alive with vermin.

The old dog's ears pricked up and he raised his head when he heard their voices. He started to wag his tail and dropped his ears but he lacked the strength to get up. The beggar looked towards the dog and a tear ran down his cheek but he quickly brushed it away and walked on. Before entering the great hall the beggar stole another glance at the dog but Argus was lying on his side – dead. The excitement had been too much for him.

Inside the hall the suitors were enjoying yet another meal at Penelope's expense. The beggar entered and sat down just inside the doorway with his back against the door post. Telemachus sent him some food and when he had eaten it he went over to the other tables to beg. All the suitors gave him food but when he reached their leader, Antinous, he was met with a hail of abuse.

The old beggar backed away and accused Antinous of being mean with food that was not even his. Antinous turned crimson and hurled a stool at him. It hit the old man on the right shoulder but he did not even flinch. He merely shook his head and returned to his place. The suitors were rather worried by the beggar's reaction and they urged Antinous to be careful; it was just possible that the old man was one of the gods in disguise.

Impending doom

The banquet was almost over when another beggar, a massive brute called Irus, turned up on the door step. He considered the palace to be his own private territory and determined to get rid of his rival. Antinous was delighted when he saw Irus trying to shove the older beggar out and urged him on. Then he got a better idea and insisted that the two beggars fight for some of the food roasting over the fire.

The older beggar rose slowly to his feet. Somehow he seemed bigger than they had expected – much broader in the chest and shoulders. The servants tucked up his tattered tunic revealing his broad muscular thighs. When Irus saw him he lost some of his confidence but he was urged on by the suitors who threatened to have him mutilated if he refused to fight.

The servants pushed Irus towards the old beggar and both men raised their fists. Irus lunged at the old man but as he came forward the beggar hit him on the back of the head. It was a murderous blow. Irus slumped to the floor with a groan and blood trickled from his mouth. The old beggar grabbed him by the ankle and dragged him out.

When the beggar returned one of the young suitors brought him a drink and spoke kindly to him. The old man felt sorry for him and tried to warn him of the danger he was in. But the young man did not hear or did not understand. His fate was sealed.

The old man's victory had gained him the grudging respect of a few of the suitors but the majority continued to abuse him. Several of the maids had fallen in with the suitors. Now even one of these joined in:

'You stupid old tramp,' she swore at him, 'why don't you get out and cause trouble somewhere else?'

The beggar's eyes hardened but he held his tongue.

Soon after sunset the party broke up and the suitors went home. Only Telemachus and the old man remained. The beggar looked over to the rack of weapons on the wall and told Telemachus to remove them. When the weapons were stored away Telemachus retired for the night leaving the old man alone.

Penelope had been waiting for this moment. She had been informed of the afternoon's events. She entered the hall with her maids, sat down and ordered that a chair be brought up for the beggar. She was curious about this old man whose actions did not match his appearance. She demanded to know who he was and where he came from.

The old man began by telling her that he came from Crete where he had met Odysseus at the beginning of the war. Penelope interrupted him before he went any further. She had heard this sort of story before and she challenged the old man to prove it. Much to her surprise he could describe Odysseus in every detail and she was forced to accept that he had met her husband. The thought of him brought tears to her eyes.

'Don't cry,' the old man begged her. 'I swear that Odysseus is alive and he is on his way home.'

Still Penelope would not believe it even though two entirely independent reports, the stranger's from Pylos and the beggar's, had sworn to the fact.

Penelope saw no point in cross-examining him further. She called over the old nurse, Eurycleia, and told her to wash the old man's feet before he went to bed. The old woman, who had been Odysseus' nurse when he was a child, went off to get a basin of warm water. The beggar watched her go and turned his back to the fire so that his face was in the shadows.

Eurycleia knelt at his feet and began to wash his legs. Suddenly her body stiffened and she let out a gasp as she felt a jagged scar above his knee. She turned to call Penelope but the beggar stopped her. The old woman smiled at him fondly and kept her knowledge to herself.

The old nurse's body stiffened and she let out a gasp as she felt the jagged scar above his knee.

...p...ers a challenge

The old beggar rose early and watched the servants going about their duties. Eumaeus came over and joined him. He had an old friend, Philoetius, with him and the three of them stood chatting in the shade. Melanthius also came into the courtyard with some choice goats for the suitors' next meal. He was the herdsman who had kicked the beggar on his way into town the previous day. When he saw the old man he again shouted abuse at him. The old beggar stiffened but he managed to control his temper.

The suitors began to arrive. They were preoccupied with their plans to murder Telemachus and oblivious of the shadow of death hanging over them. Telemachus seated the beggar near the entrance and warned the suitors to leave him alone. His tone worried them. He seemed to have gained authority since his return from Sparta. But they were not deterred. One of them hurled a cow's hoof at the old man who ducked just in time. Telemachus turned on the suitors and threatened them. They fell silent for a moment but they were soon at it again.

The uproar came to an abrupt end when Penelope entered carrying Odysseus' great hunting bow. She told her astonished suitors that she intended to settle the question of her marriage once and for all. 'Athena appeared to me last night,' Penelope began, her beautiful face betraying signs of resignation, 'and told me to decide this matter by an archery contest. All you have to do is string my husband's bow and shoot an arrow through a line of twelve axes, as he used to do before the war.'

Telemachus chuckled to himself. He doubted that any of them could even string the great bow. He jumped to his feet and set up the axes in a long line. Then he set an example by trying to string the bow himself. On his fourth attempt he almost succeeded but the old beggar caught his eye and shook his head almost imperceptably.

One by one the suitors tried their skill but they all failed. They tried warming and waxing the bow to make it more pliable but still none of them could string it. While they were struggling with the bow Eumaeus and his friend Philoetius slipped out of the hall and the beggar followed them. A short time later they returned one by one. All was now prepared.

When none of the suitors could string the bow their leader, Antinous, suggested that they put off the contest until the following day and offer sacrifices to Apollo, the archer god. Then the god could decide who should marry the queen.

It was a chance to save face and they all agreed. But their complacency was shattered when the old beggar asked if he could have a go.

The outraged suitors ridiculed the old man. 'How can he think of marrying the queen?'. Penelope cut them short.

'I am sure that the old man has no intention of carrying me off should he win,' she insisted. 'He just wants to try his skill.'

But Eurymachus, Antinous' partner in crime, refused even to consider the matter.

'And what if by some chance he should succeed,' Eurymachus retorted, 'he would make the rest of us look ridiculous.'

Penelope refused to back down and offered the beggar a reward if he could do it.

Telemachus now took over. 'It is my right as Odysseus' son to decide this matter,' he said. 'Mother, please go to your quarters.'

Penelope was shaken by his tone but she did as she was told.

Eumaeus picked up the bow and arrows and started towards the beggar. The suitors hurled abuse at him. The old swineherd faltered and dropped the bow.

'Go on,' Telemachus ordered.

Amidst uproar Eumaeus picked up the bow again and placed it in the beggar's hands. He then left the hall to look for the old nurse Eurycleia. He told her to lock herself and all the other maids away and stay there no matter what she heard. At the same time his friend Philoetius slipped out and barred the door to the courtyard.

Meanwhile the old tramp was twisting the bow lovingly between his fingers. The suitors' anger turned to laughter as they watched him. Suddenly their laughter died as they saw him effortlessly loop the string over the end and twang it. He picked up an arrow and without moving from his stool sent it singing through the axes. Not one did it touch. Odysseus was home!

Suddenly their laughter died away as they saw the old tramp string the bow. Athena watched and smiled happily. The last of the heroes, her favourite, was about to reclaim his kingdom.

The final reckoning

Telemachus grabbed his sword and spear and joined the beggar. He had known his father's identity ever since they had spent the day together in Eumaeus' cottage. The king threw off his filthy cloak and seized the quiver full of arrows. They had to make the most of the surprise for the suitors had still not recognised him. His first arrow struck Antinous in the throat and his wine cup clattered to the floor. The suitors still failed to understand what was happening. They thought it was some dreadful accident. Odysseus soon put them right.

They turned white with fear. At first Eurymachus tried to throw all the blame on Antinous. But when he realized that Odysseus intended to kill them all he drew his sword and called upon his comrades to charge in mass. He dashed forward as he spoke but Odysseus' second arrow caught him in the chest and he fell scattering the tables and crockery.

Telemachus leapt in and killed another of the suitors. He then made a dash for the storeroom which was just off the hall, to get armour and weapons. He supplied Eumaeus and Philoetius with helmets and put on one himself while his father covered them. Odysseus held his position as long as the arrows lasted. Then he stepped back into the doorway, put on a helmet and seized a shield and spears.

But now the suitors were armed too. Telemachus had left the storeroom door unlocked and Melanthius the abusive herdsman had managed to get some armour and weapons for them. Odysseus' heart sank. Although the great hall was littered with dead bodies, they were still massively outnumbered. Eumaeus, seeing Melanthius creeping back to the storeroom for more, dashed after him and locked the foul-mouthed bully in.

The suitors were trapped in the palace. There was only one way out and Odysseus was blocking it. There could be no escape until he was removed. Six of them dashed forward and hurled their spears at him. He parried them all and yelled to Telemachus and the herdsmen to throw their spears into the midst of them. The counter-attack brought down four of the suitors. They charged again desperately trying to get Odysseus but more of them fell in the exchange of spears.

Urged on by Athena, Odysseus plunged into the crowd. The suitors scattered before him and he struck them down as they ran. Their priest threw his arms around Odysseus' knees but the king showed no mercy. The court minstrel would have suffered the same fate if Telemachus had not saved him. The court herald was also spared but all the others were cut down.

When the massacre was over Odysseus sent for his old nurse and ordered her to name all the maids who had been disloyal. The nurse listed twelve of them. They were ordered to clear the bodies from the hall. When it had been thoroughly cleaned and washed down Telemachus herded them outside and hanged all twelve. They then dragged Melanthius out of the storeroom and horribly mutilated him.

At last it was over. Odysseus fumigated the palace with sulphur and then sent for Penelope and the other maids. The women came down from their quarters and threw their arms around his neck. When Penelope arrived she did not hug him as the maids had. She did not even touch him. She sat in a chair near the fire looking at him. For a long while she sat there in silence her eyes searching for the man she loved.

Telemachus grew angry with his mother but Odysseus understood her uncertainty. He told his son to leave them alone. He took a bath and put on clean clothes.

'What other wife would refuse to embrace her husband after an absence of nineteen years,' he asked her. He then turned to the old nurse and told her to make up a separate bed for him.

Penelope saw her chance.

'Bring up the king's big bed,' she told the nurse, and place it outside my room.'

Odysseus turned on her angrily:

'Who has moved my bed?' he demanded to know. 'Even a skilled craftsman would find it impossible to move. It was built into that olive tree.'

Penelope's knees went weak but she managed to struggle to her feet and throw her arms around his neck. Only Odysseus could know about that bed. It was their secret. With tears rolling down her cheeks she kissed him and begged him to forgive her for not recognising him. Odysseus held her tight and wept with her.

When the suitors realized that the old man intended to kill them all, they charged in mass. But the beggar's aim was deadly. His second arrow plunged into Eurymachus' chest and he fell headlong, scattering tables and chairs.

Men, Women and Costume

Homer and the Linear B tablets

It is difficult to estimate how much of Homer's description of Mycenaean society is true and how much reflects the system of his own day.

We know that Greece was divided up into small kingdoms, as Homer says, from the Linear B tablets. It also seems certain that the king of Mycenae was the overlord of Greece. Archaeologists have uncovered more wealth from Mycenae than any other site, and it seems to have deserved Homer's epithet of 'Golden' Mycenae.

Mycenaean society

The linear B tablets show that Mycenaean society had a hierachy. It was under the overall command of the king (wanax). This term is found in Homer. Beneath the king was a second-in-command (lawagetas or leader of the people). Below the lawagetas came the hequetai (followers). These were the nobility. The kingdom of Pylos was divided into 16 boroughs each under the control of a governor (ko-re-te) who also had a second-in-command. It is hard to trace this sort of structure in Homer.

2 A wall painting from Pylos showing a huntsman wearing a short tunic with a belt. It is difficult to decide whether the dots on his tunic are purely decorative or represent some form of reinforcement, even metal scales.

3 A wall painting from Pylos showing a man wearing a long unbelted tunic. This is part of a religious procession and the man could be a priest or the dress could be a sign of rank.

1 A wall painting from Pylos showing a huntsman wearing a short tunic without a belt.

4 One of the heads from the bowl shown on page 74. In late Mycenaean times men were usually clean shaven. Beards were sometimes worn but never moustaches.

5 Model of a boot from Voula near Athens. It shows a typical rolled up toe.

A bureaucratic society

Mycenaean society was very bureaucratic. Hordes of scribes were employed to keep records of all that was produced. Records were also kept of the various professions which give us an idea of their status. A bronze-smith for example had a very high position in society and was given special tax relief. Taxes, of course, were paid in produce. There was no money as we know it.

Farming

Most of the people would have been employed on the land, as Homer implies. Wheat, barley, wool, flax and olive oil are all mentioned on the tablets. So are livestock, particularly oxen, which even have their names listed such as Darkie and Whitefoot. All these things were listed by the scribes and assessed for taxation.

Law and justice

Such a society must have had complex laws just as Egypt and Babylonia had. This is a far cry from Homer's world where the only justice seems to have been personal vengeance.

A woman's place

A woman's place was in the home. She was wife, mother and house-keeper. She did the spinning and weaving as was the custom in all primitive societies.

Slavery

Slavery was common and no doubt slaves did the menial tasks in wealthy households. Odysseus' faithful swineherd, Eumaeus, was a slave. In the Iliad the heroes are generally only interested in female slaves. Odysseus' old nurse, Eurycleia, was a slave, and so were the other palace maids.

Men's dress

In later Mycenaean art men are generally shown wearing a short tunic which occasionally has a belt. Some of the pictures from Pylos show men wearing ankle length tunics. These may be a sign of rank or of priesthood. The Sea Peoples wore a fringed kilt much the same as the women on the opposite page. These are sometimes shown in Mycenaean art particularly in the earlier period. Both the Hittites and Mycenaeans wore shoes with 'rolled up' toes. Men wore their hair long. The upper classes appear to have beards but not moustaches.

6 A Mycenaean woman wearing a traditional dress with uncovered breasts. She appears to wear three kilts. From the palace at Thebes c1375 BC.

7 A fresco from Thera showing a woman wearing a fringed kilt over her skirt.
8 Front and back of the lower half of a statuette wearing several kilts. From Mycenae.
9 How a kilt was worn, folded and tied round the waist.
10 A unique painting of a woman from Mycenae wearing a blouse under her bodice. Note the jewellery and braided hair, so typical of Mycenaean women.

11 Two crude paintings of women from Vratsi, near Tanagra in Boeotia. These women appear to have worn kilted dresses which cover the breasts. But the representation is so crude and stylized that it is impossible to be certain.

Women's dress

Fashionable women appear to have worn the same type of dress throughout the Mycenaean era. This had a full skirt with a tight fitting bodice that left the breasts uncovered.

The style originated in Crete before 1600BC and is shown on the walls of the palace at Pylos c1250 BC.

The late period

A unique painting from Mycenae (number 10) shows a woman wearing a blouse under her bodice, and the crude paintings below (number 11) suggest that at the time of the Trojan war some women at least covered their breasts. In this book mortals are shown with covered breasts and goddesses with uncovered breasts, for convenience.

The kilt

A kilt normally appears to be worn over the skirt. The best representation of this comes from Thera (left, number 7). Here it seems quite simply to be folded horizontally so that the loose threads at the top and bottom hang down. Other illustrations (numbers 6 and 8) imply that several kilts could be worn at once.

Face and hair

Mycenaean women appear to have worn make-up such as mascara, rouge and lipstick. They wore their hair very long and decorated with braids. Hats looking rather like berets are often shown (see right, number 12).

Jewellery

Mycenaean women loved jewellery often preferring quantity to quality. Earrings, necklaces, and bracelets were all very popular. Most of the surviving metal jewellery is made of gold.

12 Painting of the head of a goddess wearing a beret type of head-dress from Mycenae.

13 A gold signet ring from Kition in Cyprus. Such rings were worn by both men and women.
14 Gold finger ring from Enkomi in Cyprus.
15 Part of a gold necklace from Enkomi in Cyprus.
16 A necklace made of cornelian from Ialysus in Rhodes.
17 Blue glass necklace with faience spacer beads believed to have been found near Athens.

Dating and Domestic Life

ABOVE: **1** A bowl decorated in typical late Mycenaean style from Mycenae. LH IIIC.

BELOW: **2** A stirrup jar decorated with broad stripes and geometric patterns from near Athens. These were used for oil and wine. LH IIIC.

BELOW: **3** Long stemmed cup from Cephalonia. LH IIIC.
4 A three legged tankard decorated with fish and birds from Miletus on the west coast of Turkey. LH IIIC.
5 and **6** Typical cups from the LH IIIC period.

Dating before history

Troy was destroyed at a time for which we have no exact dates, as there was then no written history. In such a situation archaeologists have to use comparative dating; if similar things are found on two sites then the two sites must have similar dates.

Pottery dating

The commonest things found on archaeological sites are fragments of pottery. Styles of pottery change quickly making them excellent for comparative dating. The real breakthrough comes when pottery turns up in a foreign dateable context. For example, when Mycenaean pottery is found in the grave of an Egyptian pharaoh or one of his ministers. The date of that pottery would then be known. Unfortunately these things happen very seldom.

Mycenaean dating

Archaeologists call the Mycenaean era the late Helladic period. It is divided into three main sections which are numbered I, II and III. This book is really only concerned with the third period which covers roughly 1400–1150 BC. This is sub-divided into three parts A, B and C. The latest sub-period is known as Late Helladic IIIC (LH IIIC).

The destruction of Troy

Mycenaean pottery was discovered at Troy, enabling archaeologists to place the destruction of Troy VIh (see page 46) at the end of Late Helladic IIIB, and the destruction of Troy VIIa during the Late Helladic IIIC period. This may seem very complicated, but only in this way can one see what is happening in Greece at the same time, and what its material culture was.

Pylos and Troy

A very interesting result of this comparative dating is that it can be shown that Nestor's palace at Pylos was destroyed before Troy VIIa.

Pottery shapes

The three most characteristic shapes in the later Mycenaean period (Late Helladic III) were the deep bowl, left (number 1), the stirrup jar (number 2) and the stemmed cup (number 3). As the period progressed the stems of these cups became longer. Cups and tankards, very similar to modern versions, were also common.

Pottery decoration

One of the most distinctive features of late Mycenaean pottery painting is the use of broad black horizontal bands. These can be seen on examples 1, 2 and 4 on the left. The drawings on the vases are often stylized and sometimes very crude. They vary from natural motives such as sphynxes, swans, bulls etc. to decorative patterns as shown on number 2. These are usually decorated with hatching or other patterns. Very occasionally the pattern is reversed to white on black (number 8).

ABOVE: **9** An ivory comb from Mycenae. LH IIIA.

RIGHT: A decorated ivory mirror handle showing a warrior fighting a griffin, from Enkomi in Cyprus.

ABOVE: **7** A silver cup decorated with gold and black niello heads from Mycenae.

LEFT: an unguent jar decorated with white on black from Lefkandi in Euboea. LH IIIC.

Stirrup jars

The stirrup jar (left, number 2) originated in Crete in the 16th century BC but only appeared in Greece in the later Mycenaean period. It was used for storing wine and oil. It received its name from archaeologists because its handle is like a double stirrup.

Materials

Besides clay pottery, one also finds utensils made of bronze, silver and even gold. Bone, ivory and stone were also used. Mirrors with elaborately decorated ivory handles have been found, and combs made of ivory or bone, but there can be no doubt that the commonest material for these types of things would have been wood. Unfortunately wood and also leather (another very common material), survive only in very wet or very dry places.

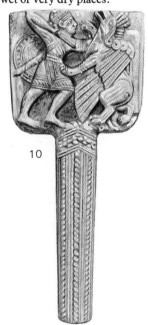

10

Food

Mycenaean food was probably nearly as varied as modern Greek food. Meat was plentiful, at least for the upper classes. The sheep and pigs mentioned by Homer are confirmed by archaeology and the Linear B tablets. Cattle were rarer. Hunting increased the variety of meat. Wild boar and deer were hunted besides smaller animals. Fish and other sea food such as octopus and shellfish, which are featured in Mycenaean art, must have been eaten.

Vegetables

Among the fruit and vegetables available were peas, beans, lentils, figs and olives (which were used to produce oil for cooking and lighting).
Flour was produced from the corn crop, and baked into bread. It is interesting that according to the Linear B tablets women ground the flour but men baked the bread.

Domestic life

Nothing is known about domestic life in Mycenaean times. Such things are not mentioned in the Linear B tablets, and the wall paintings tell us nothing either. But it cannot have been much different from the picture that Homer draws.

Furniture

Homer mentions chairs, tables and beds. The Linear B tablets add footstools. None of these have survived, but tiny models of three legged chairs have been found (number 12 below). Reconstructions of a table (11) and a bed (13) have been made from traces left in the volcanic ash on the island of Thera. These were in use about 1500 BC but there is no reason to suppose that later types differed much.

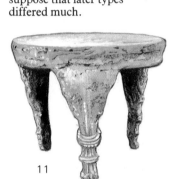

11

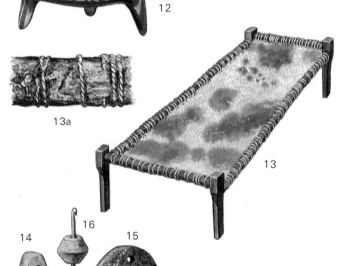

13a

14   16   15

11 A plaster cast of a table made from traces left in the volcanic ash on the island of Thera. C 1500 BC.
12 Tiny model of a three legged chair found at Mycenae.

13 A bed made from wood and hide reconstructed from traces left in the volcanic ash on the island of Thera. c 1500 BC.
13a A plaster cast of one of the sides of the bed (13). One can easily see the cords holding the hide in position.
14, 15 Two loom weights.
16 A spindle.

BELOW: a Scythian archer stringing his bow, from a gold cup. This appears to have been the type of bow used by Odysseus.

RIGHT: 1 Scythian bow (strung).
2 Scythian bow (unstrung).
3 Cretan bow (strung).

1   2

3

BELOW: a hunting scene showing a wild boar being driven onto the spears of hunters by dogs. The original wall painting which was found at Tiryns is very fragmentary.

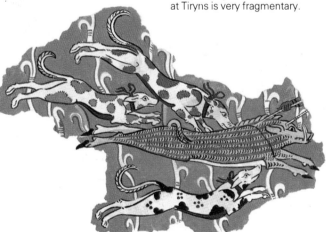

Hunting

Hunting was very popular and is often featured in Mycenaean art. The Lion hunt dagger which comes from an earlier period shows four men armed with body shields and spears, hunting a lion. Shields are not shown in later pictures, but the hunters wear linen leg-guards, a necessary precaution when hunting lions or wild boars, and they still carry spears. A fifth figure on the 'Lion Hunt' dagger carries a bow which brings us to the difficult question of Odysseus' bow.

Odysseus' Bow

In later Greek times two types of bow were used, the simple Cretan bow (above, number 3), and the more complex Scythian bow (numbers 1 and 2). Both were made of wood reinforced with horn and sinew. Only the Cretan bow seems to be shown in Mycenaean art, but the trouble that the suitors had stringing Odysseus' hunting bow suggests that it was the Scythian type, which reverses its curve when unstrung and requires the use of both hands and legs to string it.

Ithaca: The Home of Odysseus

Where was Ithaca?

The Ithaca described by Homer bears little if any resemblance to modern Ithaca.
Odysseus describes his home as one of a group of islands. This is true but he adds that it was the farthest out to sea and that it slanted towards the west.

Cephalonia?

This is a perfect description of the neighbouring and much larger island of Cephalonia. Odysseus claims that its landmark is the wooded peak of windswept Neriton. The highest point on Ithaca is Mount Anogi at 806m. Cephalonia has no less than five hills higher than Mount Anogi. The highest, Mount Ainos, is twice the height of Mount Anogi at 1628m.

Levkas or Sicily?

It is hardly surprising that many scholars have looked elsewhere for Odysseus' kingdom. Dörpfeld, who discovered Troy VI, thought it was Levkas while others argued that it was not even off the coast of Greece but that it was the western end of Sicily.

The cave of the Tripods

In spite of this there is one almost irrefutable piece of evidence that points to modern Ithaca. Odysseus had thirteen tripods with him when he returned home. He hid these away in a cave. About 1931, thirteen tripods dating to the 8th century BC were found in a cave at Polis Bay on Ithaca. No one suggests that these belonged to Odysseus but it does imply that even in Homer's own day this island was believed to be Odysseus' kingdom and that these tripods were an offering to the hero.

Where was the palace?

Most Mycenaean finds have come from the northern part of Ithaca. Between 1930 and 1932 the British archaeologist Sylvia Benton excavated along the south-east side of Mt Exogi. It was she who excavated the cave of the Tripods. She also found traces of settlements on the north side of Polis Bay and just north of Stavros, but no sign of a palace.
There is an ancient Greek tower on the eastern slope of Mount Exogi which would be an excellent site for a palace. The area is strewn with fragments of pottery proving that there was once a settlement there.

ABOVE TOP: Vathy harbour, Ithaca. Homer describes the harbour where Odysseus landed on his return home as having two bold headlands squatting at its mouth. It would be hard to describe Vathy harbour better. Mount Anogi is in the background.

ABOVE: Polis Bay seen from the south-east. Cephalonia can be seen in the background. The cave of the Tripods was about half way along the far side of the bay. The Mycenaean settlement was further up the hillside.

RIGHT: Mt Exogi seen from the south east. The main Mycenaean settlement was to the left of centre where all the houses are. The Greek tower is half way up the hillside right in the centre of the picture.

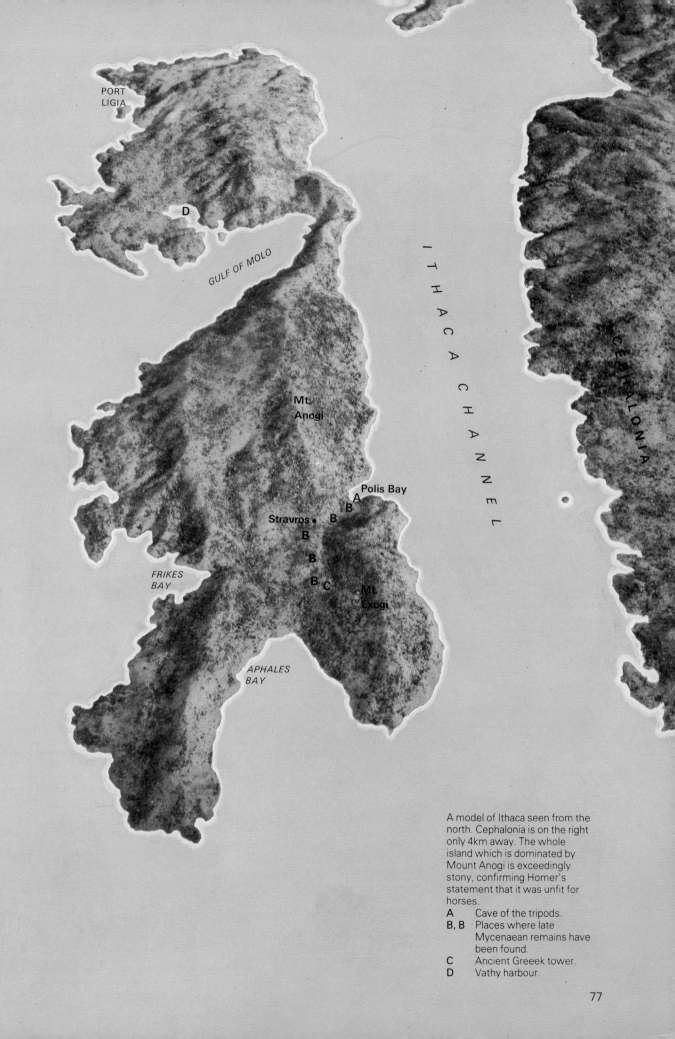

PORT
LIGIA

D

GULF OF MOLO

I T H A C A   C H A N N E L

C E P H A L O N I A

Mt.
Anogi

Polis Bay

A

B

Stravros •   B

B

B

B   C

Mt
Exogi

*FRIKES
BAY*

*APHALES
BAY*

A model of Ithaca seen from the north. Cephalonia is on the right only 4km away. The whole island which is dominated by Mount Anogi is exceedingly stony, confirming Homer's statement that it was unfit for horses.

A   Cave of the tripods.
B, B   Places where late Mycenaean remains have been found.
C   Ancient Greeek tower.
D   Vathy harbour.

The Trojan War: FACT OR FICTION?

Legend or history

There is no clear line between legend and history. The Trojan war comes in the 'no man's land' between the two. Most scholars would agree that there was a Trojan war. (It is too important a part of Greek tradition to be pure fantasy). Yet they would strenuously deny that Homer's account of it is historical in any way.

The bards

For centuries the stories of the Iliad and the Odyssey were handed down verbally from generation to generation through the bards. Each bard would add his own colour to the story placing increasing emphasis on the characters, often replacing fact with fantasy.

Finally in the 8th century BC the two great epic poems were reshaped and written down. Homer probably gave them their final form.

How much is true?

It is impossible to strip the fantasy from the truth. The sheer scale of the expedition with more than 1,000 ships and some 50,000 men involved is unbelievable. The problem of feeding such an army would be enormous. Even if it were possible they could never have stayed, winter and summer, for over nine years. Camped next to the marshes the Greek army would have been wiped out by plague long before Troy fell.

A series of raids?

It seems far more likely that the siege was merely a series of raids similar to those of the Sea Peoples. These attacks could have taken place over many years possibly involving both the sixth and seventh town. The local people would have lived in constant fear of raiders ravaging the countryside, and would have been forced to move into the town for protection. The crude shacks built against the inside of the walls, and the buried stores of food in Troy VIIa confirm this story.

Picture of a bard singing to the accompaniment of a lyre, from Pylos.

The final assault

In the end the Greeks may have decided to make an all-out effort to reduce the stronghold. The germ of this may be detected in the retreat to the island of Tenedos before the final assault. This time the Greeks came armed with siege equipment, the Trojan horse.

A battering-ram?

Many explanations of the Trojan horse have been put forward. The most likely is that it was a battering-ram. It is significant that the Greeks were inside it and that part of the wall had to be knocked down to get it into the town.

The battering-ram had been in use in the middle east since at least 2,000BC and must have been known to the Mycenaeans. This knowledge was lost in the dark age that followed the fall of Mycenae. The battering-ram did not reappear in Greece until the 5th century BC, but it remained in use in western Asia.

The impregnable walls

The massive sloping base of the wall at Troy was 4.5m thick and up to 4m high, backed up with earth. It had been specially designed to withstand battering. This must have presented the Greeks with a serious problem requiring a special machine.

Why a horse?

The name given to the machine must have reflected its shape. It would have needed a housing that could raise the ram about 4m so that it could be brought to bear on the superstructure of the wall.

In the reconstruction below the upright beams have been extended to form legs. This could be the reason it was called a horse. It was common practice in the ancient world to give such nicknames to pieces of equipment. The Romans called their catapults scorpions and onagers, and the very word 'ram' comes from the animal.

The heroes

Some of the heroes may have been historical figures. The portrayal of Agamemnon is so unflattering that it has to be based on truth. Nestor and Diomedes may also be real people.

Some such as Ajax, Hector and Achilles, may have come from a different era. Achilles with his blonde hair and his brutal practices that shocked his Greek friends, does not fit. He appears to be from a different place or time.

Achilles' armour

When Achilles put on his sacred armour he tested it 'to see if it allowed his limbs free movement'. This w___ the Dendra type of armo___ (____ 30), with its cumbersome shoulder guards and girdle plates. But it would not be necessary if he were wearing the simpler armour of Homer's day. According to legend Achilles could only be wounded in the heel. The only part of the body left unprotected by the Dendra armour was the back of the lower leg. Are these things sheer coincidence or do they betray traces of a legend far older than the Trojan war?

Odysseus

The hero of this book plays a rather unimportant role in the Iliad, a part which could well have been woven into the story later. It is possible that he comes from a later period or that he is entirely fictional.

It seems odd that no trace of his palace has been found on Ithaca. It is a tiny island only 22km long. There are not many places where a palace could have been built, and enough people have searched for it. Sylvia Benton argued that earthquakes and erosion had probably destroyed its foundations. However, substantial remains of an ancient Greek tower built on top of a small cliff on the side of Mount Exogi have survived for two and a half thousand years. If such an unstable building as a tower has survived surely something would remain of a palace.

ABOVE: a battering ram shown on an Assyrian bas relief.

BELOW: a possible reconstruction of the Trojan horse. It is raised on legs to bring the ram up to the level of the upper wall. It would be pointless battering the lower wall which is backed up with earth. The ram would be hung from the roof beam and operated by men within the housing which was covered with hides to stop the enemy setting fire to it. The machine would be moved up to the wall on rollers.

Index

Achilles, Greek hero 6, 78;
    armour of, 36, 37, 78;
    avenges Patroclus 36, 37;
    death of, 40, 41, 57;
    kills Hector 38–p;
    quarrels with Agamemnon
        10, 11, 18, 22, 24, 26;
    sails against Troy 6, 7, 8
Aegisthus 50
Aeneas 6, 20
Agamemnon, King of Mycenae
        5, 78;
    citadel of, 14–15;
    commands force against
        Troy 6, 7, 8, 18, 42;
    death of, 50, 57;
    murder avenged 53;
    quarrel with Achilles 10, 11,
        22, 24, 36;
    shield of, 32;
    wounded 25
Ajax, Prince of Salamis 6, 7,
        24, 57, 78;
    death of, 41;
    duel with Hector 22, 23, 32;
    in battle 26, 27, 36, 40;
    shield of, 32;
Antenor 9, 43
Antinous 65, 66, 68, 70
Aphrodite 20, 34, 38;
    the judgement of Paris 5, 11,
        19, 41
Apollo 34, 68;
    avenges his priest 10;
    fights for Troy 11, 20, 26,
        36, 37, 38, 40
Archaeology:
    dating 74;
    sites:
        Athens 32, 73, 74;
        Dendra 29, 30, 32, 78;
        Enkomi 12, 29, 32, 33, 73,
            74;
        Hagia Triada 33, 34, 35;
        Hattusa 12;
        Kallithea 31, 32;
        Kaloriziki 12, 32;
        Knossos 28, 33;
        Tarsus 12, 29, 31;
        Thebes, Egypt 12, 30;
        Tiryns 12, 28, 29, 75;
        Ugarit 12, 29
    see also Medinet Habu
            Mycenae
            Pylos
            Thera
Ares 21, 22, 34, 38
Armour 28–32;
    Dendra 30, 32, 78
Artemis 34
Athena 34;
    aids Odysseus 18, 52, 69, 70;

battle among the gods 38;
    fights for the Greeks 11, 20,
        21, 24;
    judgement of Paris 5;
    offended by Greeks 43, 50;
    restrains Achilles 10;
    saves Achilles 38, 39;
    wooden horse 42

Benton, Sylvia
    British archaeologist 76, 78
Briseis 10
Burial rites 35

Calypso 59
Cassandra of Troy 42, 43
Chariots in battle 33
Charybdis 58, 59, 61
Cyclops 54–5, 56

Deiphobus 41, 42, 43
Diomedes, King of Argos 6,
        36, 50, 78;
    in battle 20–24, 25
Dorpfeld, Wilhelm 46, 76

Egyptian Empire 12, 72
Eumaeus 64, 65, 69, 70, 72
Eurycleia 66, 69, 72
Eurymachus 68, 70

Hades 34
Hector, champion of Troy 6, 8,
        21, 22, 78;
    death of, 39, 40;
    duel with Ajax 22, 23, 32;
    in battle 24, 25, 26, 27;
    kills Patroclus 36;
    last fight 38–9;
    shames Paris 18, 19;
    shield of, 32
Helen, cause of war 9, 23;
    duel for, 18, 19;
    marries Deiphobus 41, 42;
    oath, the 5;
    returned to Ménelaus 43, 53
Hephaestus 34, 36
Hera 11, 20, 21, 34
Hittites 12, 32, 72
Homer 12, 15;
    heroes of, 7, 28, 31;
    Illiad, The 12, 29, 32, 33, 34,
        35, 60, 72, 78;
    Mycenae of, 72;
    Odyssey, The 12, 60, 61, 76,
        78;
    ships of, 16, 17;
    Troy of, 45, 46, 47, 48
Irus 66
Ithaca 4, 61, 76–7

Kadesh, battle of 12, 32, 33

Laestrygonians, land of 56, 61
Laocoon 42

Malea, Cape of 6, 50, 51, 61
Medinet Habu, Egypt
    temple reliefs 12, 13, 17, 28
Melanthius 65, 68, 70
Menelaus, King of Sparta 5,
        53, 54;
    duel with Paris 18, 19;
    in battle 26, 36, 41;
    reclaims Helen 43;
    sails for home 50;
    speaks to Trojans 8, 9;
    summons heroes 6, 7
Mycenae:
    citadel 14–15;
    lion hunt dagger 32, 75;
    site 12, 34, 72, 73, 74;
    Treasury of Atreus 35;
    warrior vase 28, 29, 31, 32
Mycenaen:
    empire 12;
    life and times 72–5, 78;
    palace 62–3;
    religion 34, 35;
    settlements 13;
    ships 16, 17;
    warriors 28–33;
    writing 12, 31, 33, 34, 72, 75
Myrmidons 36

Nestor, King of Pylos 6, 10, 22,
        24, 78;
    in the Iliad 34;
    palace of 62, 74;
    sails home 50;
    son killed 40

Odysseus, King of Ithaca 4;
    bow of, 75;
    fall of Troy 43;
    Iliad 29;
    in battle 25, 26, 40, 41;
    oath, the 5, 6, 7;
    return of, 52, 64–70;
    sails for home 50, 51;
    ships of, 17;
    speaks to Trojans 8–9;
    story of, 54–59;
    Trojan war 18, 19, 22, 24,
        36;
    voyages of, 60–1;
    wooden horse 42

Orestes 50, 53

Pandarus 20
Paris, Prince of Troy:
    death of, 41;
    duel with Menelaus 18, 19,
        20;
    for love of Helen 5, 23;
    judgement of, 5, 11;
    no hero 6, 40
Patroclus, friend of Achilles,
        41, 57;

avenged 39, 40;
    slaying of 36–37
Penelope, wife of Odysseus 4,
        52, 64–70
Phi and Psi figures 34
Philoetius 68, 69, 70
Posiedon 26, 34, 55, 56
Priam, King of Troy 19, 38, 40,
        42
Pylos:
    bronze weapons 17–19;
    catastrophe 12;
    Linear B tablets 12, 34, 72,
        75;
    Nestor's palace 62–3, 74;
    wall paintings 28, 29, 32, 33,
        72, 73, 78

Religion 34–5

Schliemann, Heinrich,
        discoverer of Troy 12, 45,
        46, 47
Scylla 58, 59, 61
Sea Peoples 72;
    armour 17, 28, 29, 31, 32;
    invasions of, 12, 13, 17, 78
Sinon and the wooden horse 42
Sirens 58, 61

Teiresias 56, 57, 58
Telemachus, Odysseus's son
        65, 66, 68, 69, 70;
    the search 52–3; 54, 64
Thera, volcanic island 75;
    frescos 16, 73
Thetis 6, 10, 11, 36, 40
Thrinacie, island of, 56, 58
Trojan War 12, 33, 45, 78;
    legend 8–11, 18–27, 36, 43
Troy:
    bronze weapons 31;
    destruction of, 74, 78;
    excavation 46–7;
    Homer's Troy 46, 47;
    plain of, 44–5;
    ruins discovered 12;
    siege of 48–49
    VIIa 46, 48, 49, 74, 78

Uranus 34

Warriors 28–33
Warrior vase see Mycenae
Weapons 28, 31, 32, 75
Wooden Horse 42–43, 78

Zeus 18, 24, 34, 40;
    avenges Achilles 10, 11;
    interferes in Trojan war 20,
        21, 24, 26, 38, 40;
    thunderer 23, 24, 26

Oxford University Press, Walton Street, Oxford OX2 6DP

Oxford   New York   Toronto
Delhi   Bombay   Calcutta   Madras   Karachi
Petaling Jaya   Singapore   Hong Kong   Tokyo
Nairobi   Dar es Salaam   Cape Town

and associated companies in
Berlin   Ibadan

Oxford is a trade mark of Oxford University Press

© Peter Connolly 1986

First published in the United States in 1988

Acknowledgements and thanks to Dr Reynold Higgens
for reading over the text

British Library Cataloguing in Publication Data
Connolly, Peter
    The Legend of Odysseus.
    I. Title   II. Homer. Odysseus.
    823'.914(F)   PZ7
    ISBN   0–19–917065–7

Library of Congress catalog card number: 88-42992

Phototypeset by Oxford Publishing Services
Printed in Hong Kong